WHEN ALASKA WAS FREE

by

KNUT D. PETERSON

shley Books, Inc.
Port Washington, N. Y. 11050

Published simultaneously in Canada by George J. McLeod,
Limited, 73 Bathurst Street, Toronto, Ontario M5V 2P8

WHEN ALASKA WAS FREE © Copyright 1977, by Knut D. Peterson

Library of Congress Number: 77-70299
ISBN: 0-87949-081-0

Address information to Ashley Books, Inc.,
Box 768, Port Washington, New York 11050

Published by Ashley Books, Inc.
Manufactured in the United States of America

Dedicated to the men and women who love the outdoors, Nature, and her out-of-the-way hidden beauty, her silent peace, wild life, and endless surprises.

INTRODUCTION

This book was written by an Alaskan sourdough from the last frontier. It is told exactly as he would tell it to you if you were sitting alongside him in front of your fireplace or out in the woods by a campfire, enjoying the freedom of the Alaskan wilderness.

CONTENTS

CONTENTS

FOREWORD

A note of explanation to the reader is appropriate, for this book contains anecdotes about actual experiences. Many are humorous, a few tragic, and though some may read like fiction, all are accounts of actual happenings. If the humorous side of life has been emphasized, it is because I feel that humor has an important place in everyone's life. We may lose everything we own in the way of money and property, but if we still have our sense of humor and good health, we haven't really lost anything.

However, all of my experiences on the Alaskan frontier have not been humorous. For instance, being torn up by a big grizzly and subsequently spending a year in the hospital was far from being something to laugh at, yet the doctors told me that if it had not been for my sense of humor they doubted very much that I would have pulled through.

Besides, had it not been for that experience, this book would never have been written. I was more or less helpless for a couple of years, so I had time to do a lot of thinking and writing. But I'm really an outdoorsman, and my writing ability amounts to just the way I would relate an experience to you in the shade of a tree, or on a cold night, beside the fireplace. So, realizing this, I hope you will enjoy my stories of the Alaskan frontier. Maybe you'll even catch the fragrance of coffee brewing over a spruce fire, or hear the crack of the ice on a freezing wintry night as you read along. Come and let me introduce you to the Alaska of an old sourdough who loves it.

CHAPTER ONE

WARM WELCOME

It was a cold blustery day in November, 1923, when I landed in Cordova on the old steamship Victoria. I warmed right up, despite the weather, and it seemed like a voice within me said: Here you are, my boy, this is the place you have been looking for. In a few hours I felt like I had stumbled into a bunch of friends that I had known for a long time, and that I was one of their long-lost brothers for whom they had been searching for years.

Old sourdoughs on the dock were talking about the good old days, about working their placer gold mines, trap lines, or prospecting for gold, or, as they called it, pay streaks. They recalled thawing their way through frozen stream-worn gravel and digging holes to bedrock. I heard them saying, ten cent pans, two bit pans, dollar pans, so much a yard, so much a foot on bedrock. It was all new to me, but it was interesting to listen to. I also heard them say that lots of moose and caribou still lived in the woods, fish in the lakes and streams, mountain sheep on the hills

1

and lots of birds, ducks and geese in the clear air. Help yourself to what you need, all is yours, and you are welcome, was their philosophy.

I only had a few dollars in my pocket, and there was no work in Cordova at that time of the year. I wasn't too sure just how things would turn out. In the club pool hall I got to talking to a man who said his name was Knut Nafstead, and when I told him that I had just come in on the boat and that I had to get work pretty soon, I didn't even get a chance to say any more. He took over.

"Oh hell," he said, "you're worried about being out of work and out of money? You're in Alaska now, and here we make it a rule to live and forget about worry. You're better off here broke, than in Seattle with a hundred dollars in your pocket.

"Do you see that lunch counter and restaurant in the back end of this pool hall? Well, that's my restaurant, and I'll give you a meal ticket for as long as you stay here in Cordova. Pay me when you can. About the only work available now is in the Kennicott Copper mine, and if you go to the railroad depot and see the agent, I am sure he'll send you up on the next train. Come on with me over to the lunch counter and I'll get you a meal ticket. If you do go to work in the mine, you can pay me in the spring when you come down, or send it to me. I'll get you a room too, and all will be taken care of, so keep your few dollars in your pocket." After a big meal, and a meal ticket in my name under the counter, he took me to a nice room. "Have a good sleep," he said. "See you tomorrow."

That night when I went to bed I asked myself why the hell I hadn't come up here years ago. I had never met so many friendly people in a small town anywhere. I told

2

myself that I thought I would be in Alaska for a long time, and sure enough, more than fifty years later I am still here.

If it was possible even today to come to a town like Cordova was in 1923, and get off the boat for a few hours during unloading of freight, a lot of us would go back to the boat, get our baggage, and say, to hell with it all, this is where I settle down.

CHAPTER TWO

THE TRAIL BLAZERS

Outdoorsmen of the A - 1 class, gold miners, prospectors, traders, trappers, fishermen, adventure-seeking trail blazers, and strong, healthy, red-blooded men of many nationalities, were the first pioneers who invaded Alaska after it became United States real estate.

They were an average lot, and had two things in common: guts and the desire to cut loose from their low-paying, tied-down jobs. They were tired of hard labor, ten and twelve hour shifts on heavy construction, pick and shovel work, poor accommodations, low wages, hard-boiled foremen, and pace setters. In short, slave drivers!

So as soon as they heard that Seward had made a deal with Russia for the so-called "ice-box", a lot of good men dropped their picks and shovels and told the bosses and pace setters what they could do with their jobs. It was bad for the contractors, but good for Alaska, because it took men like these to enter a distant country almost bare-handed, a country as wild, cold and unknown as Alaska was then.

CHAPTER THREE

THE TERRITORY OF ALASKA

In the years before statehood, Alaska consisted of a few small towns and villages, scattered far and wide throughout a huge unpopulated area. Any stranger in any town or village was always met with open arms and friendly smiles, and made to feel at home before he had a chance to start worrying about tomorrow. After a few months in Alaska, you began to realize that you were at home, and I mean the territory of Alaska was home, no matter where you happened to be; on lonely trails or countless miles away. It was always home. Alaska was the biggest home in the world, and its people were like one big family, both natives and whites, each following whatever appealed to him.

In some places in the interior, your next door neighbor was from twenty to fifty miles or more, but even so, you usually called on each other once in a while, but not just to say hello. It would be a visit of at least a week or two. There was no hurry. Everybody had lots of time to visit. Friendship, sociability, and concern were common all over Alaska. The natives always kept track of white prospectors out in the hills. They didn't tell you that they came out there to see if all was well, but that was mostly what it was. They would tell you, oh, we wanted to make a trip just to see if there was any sign of big game, and maybe we hunt out this way later on. If you happened to be out of meat, they would hunt from your camp, leave you some meat, and have meat for their trip back. In short, they were a real social part of the big family with whom we all shared that big home called the territory of Alaska.

The Kennicott mine and the Alaska Road Commission were about the only work in the interior in those days where you could always go and make some money if you had to. A lot of people made a go of it without working for anybody—placer mining, trapping and prospecting. With the natives, it was mostly hunting, fishing, trapping, and some road work, and of course a lot of canneries along the coast.

The old timers from territorial days feel more like strangers in their own homes or towns and they'll never be as happy as they were in those days when people were few and far between. Those were the days when there was no welfare, no unemployment compensation, no social security, no food stamps, and no hand outs of any kind. Each person depended on himself. There was nothing else to depend on, although you could always count on plenty of friends willing to assist you in case of misfortune. You might borrow or loan out some beans and flour on and off, but it was always returned with good measure. Fur was fairly high-priced, but otherwise there was no big money in circulation. Money was no problem anyway. Nobody had a hell of a lot of it, most of us worked for wages part of the time, but on our own most of the time.

There were no supermarkets then. The towns had a few stores, for clothing, shoes, groceries and hardware, and throughout the interior there were quite a lot of well-stocked trading posts. If you decided to spend a winter on some creek, prospecting by sinking holes to bedrock, thawing your way through frozen stream gravel, and maybe doing some trapping at the same time, and your problem was no money, you could usually go to a trader and tell him that you needed a ton of grub and dog food, but were unable to pay for it just now. The answer would be, make out your list and I'll fix you right up. So you took off on the first snow, freighting in your outfit to your winter quarters, set up your tent, and maybe built a small cabin. At any rate, you were busy, working, singing most of the time, thinking that sure as hell you'd find a good pay streak before the winter was over, happy as a lark, busy as a beaver, partner or no partner. You were on your own, working for yourself, cutting wood for thawing frozen ground and for the camp, digging, cooking for yourself and for your dogs, feeding dogs, washing and patching clothes, making trips with the dog team, setting tending to traps, skinning stretching and drying fur. A good thing you were busy, too, as you had very little reading material, radio, or any other kind of entertainment, and of course no communication of any kind, which could be bad if something went wrong. But you were too busy to worry about it. You were there because you wanted to be there, and so you were contented. Before you knew it, spring was right close by, and what happened? Maybe you found pay dirt and would try mining the creek. Maybe you caught enough fur to pay for your outfit, and maybe you failed on both

7

counts. Anyway you had lots of fun. If it didn't pan out, there were lots of other places to go. Just now you were due for a little spring vacation. So most likely you would head for some lakes, trap a bunch of muskrats, and see a lot of other people, including some young native girls. At any rate, all is well, and there is nothing to worry about. Alaska is free and open, and wherever you go it's all yours, and you are sure of a welcome.

An old friend of mine explained it this way. When Alaska was a territory, everybody was as free as a bird in the air. Since it has become a state, we're all as free as a bird in a cage.

CHAPTER FOUR

THE STATE OF ALASKA

Alaska became a state in 1959, and it is doubtful whether any piece of real estate on this planet ever changed as fast as this biggest state in the Union did. From a few small towns and villages (the result of military installations during World War II), a narrow graded road, mining camps, pack trails, dog trails, trap lines, and endless wilderness, it now boasts cities, paved highways, big airports with scheduled flights for almost any country in the world, lots of producing oil wells, and farming on formerly wild land. Right now construction is underway on the 800 mile pipe line from the north slope oil field to Valdez. It is all big deals today and they call it progress. I wonder if it really is.

The territory of Alaska was big; you're damn right it was big. It wasn't all cut up like the state is today. Many good people came here intending to get a small tract of land to build a home on, only to find that this big state is locked up. There is no place to go. There is not enough land to go around. In the old days the territory belonged to whoever

9

happened to make his camp or home here, but now we sort of wonder who it does belong to. One thing we do know. The state is well stocked with law makers, and so we're getting more and more new laws, rules, and restrictions every year. By now this big state consists of all kinds of restricted areas, such as military reserves, Indian reservations, native land grants, wild life reserves, and many other kinds of reserves. It appears that the interior of Alaska has all been locked up for some sort of reserve, and there it will lie from now on, and for what? Do the reserve-happy law makers, politicians, or whatever handle we're supposed to give them, know the mountain ranges in Alaska, with their heavily mineralized zones of untold wealth? Do they know they have locked the door to men who really want to do something to develop the state, and make something out of it in the way of producing not only gold, but base metal of all kinds? Now that the oil companies are tapping Alaska's oil, why lock up her hidden wealth in minerals? And why all the reserves with all their rules and restrictions?

Although Alaska may have been progressing in many other ways, this, in my opinion, is making progress in reverse. The government spent millions of dollars on geological surveys to map out the many different formations in order to show where the most likely mineral bearing districts could be found. Now with all the reserves and restricted areas, how can anyone get to the mineral deposits and mine them? In the goldrush days Alaska was known as the Northern Frontier, then the last frontier. Now it has become the lost frontier, or maybe we should say the locked up frontier, consisting of millions and millions of lonesome acres out there on big lonesome reserves.

CHAPTER FIVE

THE GOOD THINGS

I can't leave the subject of statehood though without commenting on what deserves praise and good words. Since 1959 a lot of consideration has been given to the pioneers of Alaska. New pioneer homes have been built, and the best of care given to the old-timers who have been in Alaska a certain length of time. A longevity bonus of one hundred dollars a month is awarded each old timer at the age of 65. Considering the endless spiralling of inflation, this means a lot to us older men and women with our limited incomes and rising prices.

In territorial days the pioneer home at Sitka was the only place for the old-timers to go to when they got too old to take care of themselves. Many of them preferred to stay in their own cabins as long as they possibly could and actually a lot of them passed away alone in their cabins, in most cases at a very old age. Some of the old pioneers lived in odd places, usually in good cabins, but away from any towns or roads. No doubt it was a terribly lonesome life for

11

them, but they had been there so long they felt lost away from their own place. Hunting for meat in the fall, cutting wood, cooking, washing, darning, and all the other chores, kept them in good healthy condition, and they usually had a dog or two for company.

Now, with the many paved highways throughout Alaska, quite a few of the old retired Alaskans own some sort of home along the way. Several of them have a car, or pickup to get around with, visit friends and do their shopping, and some get on a plane in the fall and go to the lower States for the winter months to visit friends or relatives, or just be in a milder climate. While their lives may be sort of on the lonesome side, it is nothing compared with the pioneer of the territory. Today's old timer, even if he lives in his own quarters, has a radio, and in many cases, television, lots of reading material, and in most places along the highway mail comes at least twice a week, or even every day. But he knows that if he does get tired of putting up with it alone, he can go to the pioneers' home. It cheers the old-timers up to know that just because they have seen a lot of years go by, they are not forgotten by the state they helped shape.

CHAPTER SIX

PROSPECTING AND GOLD MINING

When people hear and read about the big gold stampedes, the big placer mining camps, and the millions of dollars in gold they produced, they get the idea that all the streams containing enough gold to be worth mining have been worked out, and there is no more placer gold to look for in Alaska. Nothing could be farther from the truth. Some day a lot of it will be discovered and mined, providing our state government makes it possible for prospectors to go out there in the hills to look for it, without having to wonder how they can get there without getting lost in all the reserves, land grants or reservations, and if they can wash a pan of gravel without being accused of muddying the water and killing a lot of fish, or getting mud in their eyes. It appears that all the over-ambitious ecologists are not too well posted on many of nature's activities. They evidently don't know that a couple of days of flood water in a big part of Alaska will carry more mud in to streams and rivers than all the placer mining operations on this planet for all

13

time could possibly produce.

With all the placer mining in Alaska the last hundred years, isn't it a miracle that any fish have survived? While fish may be valuable, gold has become more valuable. Instead of from $16 to $35 an ounce, gold is now from $100 to $160 an ounce, and it may stabilize at about $150 an ounce. Of course, until they do stabilize it, there is no guarantee as to its dependable value.

A lot of creeks in Alaska are what we refer to as wet creeks. They don't freeze dry, as there is live water slipping through the gravel, making it impossible to dig a hole to bedrock. Many attempts were made by the old timers to freeze down, but they seldom worked. They had to give it up and walk away from it knowing that the formation was right, and a good possibility for pay dirt. But it takes a drill to prospect and test the ground, and that was too expensive for them to think about. A lot of those creeks are scattered throughout Alaska, and maybe some day somebody will be out there drilling on some of them, and find all kinds of pay dirt. Or maybe they will be left just as they are, clear water freely flowing for the fish to swim in.

This is the age of equipment and while good prospectors may not be financially strong enough to buy drilling equipment and tractors, there are lots of men in Alaska today with enough capital to back reliable prospectors on whatever terms they may agree to. Many pay streaks were found that way in the old days; grub stalking they called it. One party put up the outfit, and the other party, or parties, went out in the field to search for the pay dirt. There's still lots of money out there on the bedrock of the many wet creeks.

With hard rock prospectors it's a matter of getting

14

out to where the formation is favorable, and now, with much of the land in the reserves, this may be a problem. Copper at a dollar a pound should be worth while looking for. Over six hundred million dollars worth of copper came out of the Kennicott mine in Alaska at 16 to 28 cents a pound. Other copper deposits will be found in Alaska if they ever decide to let people go out there and look for them. They say the big mining companies have been all over the mineralized zones with planes and helicopters with powerful detectors and instruments to tell them all about what is in the ground below. Maybe so, but I don't buy that. I have a lot more confidence in the hard rock prospector following the foot hills, and watching for signs of ore; walking up and down the gulches and keeping it up day after day; picking likely looking samples and breaking them with his hammer. After many dull days a sample breaks in many pieces, and Wow! he says to himself, look here, I'll be god-damned if that ain't gold. Them little specks sparkling here and there throughout the broken pieces of rock. So he crushes it down and pans it, and sure enough, there they are, glaring at him from the gold pan. There is no mistake, so he moves his camp right over to the gulch, because he knows he'll be working there for some time trying to trace the vein the pieces broke off from.

As for the hard rock deposits in Alaska, there is no reason why they shouldn't exist. But who is out looking for them? Nobody! Over on the Canadian side, they find one new deposit after another. New mines are going into production every year. How come? Well, the Canadians are out there prospecting. If that wasn't so, they wouldn't find anything either. One big copper deposit in Alaska, over in the Kobuck Country, has been found, tested, and sold for three million dollars. It would still be unknown if somebody hadn't gone out there and proved to the world that there are big mineral deposits in Alaska waiting for somebody to discover them.

CHAPTER SEVEN

PLACER GOLD

Mining for placer gold is a job for a strong, healthy man. It always seems to run into a lot of hard work, but if a person likes it well enough, he forgets all about the hard work and keeps at it till he is tired and then rests and sleeps 'til he is well rested. He enjoys his work. To him, it's lots of fun, especially if he has a few claims of his own and the ground is good enough to keep him from going to work for somebody else.

There are no heavy expenses to contend with in order to operate, it doesn't really take such an awful lot of gold to make a go of it. There are many ways of mining for placer gold. For instance, what we call open-cut mining involves stripping off all the overburden of earth either with water or machinery. Water, of course, is the cheapest method. Hydraulic pipe line can be used, or if the ground is not too deep, it can be washed off with what we call a boom dam. A dam is built across the creek ten or twelve feet high with a spillway and automatic gate which will open when the dam is full, and close automatically when the

17

water is all out of it. As the gate opens and lets out the big pond of water, it washes the dirt, gravel and rocks on down the stream. This is the cheapest way of stripping off overburden. A lot of stripping is done with the bulldozers now. And in a lot of places where they mine with 'dozers, the oil companies and equipment dealers get most, if not all, of the money.

For instance, a couple of good miners could mine out a small creek with a boom dam in eight or ten years and make a pretty good profit. A man with a good 'dozer will mine it in two or three years and lose money doing it. Of course, there are places that it's the other way around; where a 'dozer will do the work and show a profit, but working it by hand just couldn't be done. Water, of course, is a big factor. Some places you have too much and other places not enough. But wherever water can be put to work expenses will be light.

Then we have what we call drift mining. This is thawing the frozen ground along the bedrock and wheeling the dirt out of a tunnel on a high bench, or hoisting it up a shaft, putting the waste in one pile and the pay dirt in another. This is usually done in the wintertime. Then when the water comes in the spring, you sluice your pay dirt, and if your poke is heavy enough, you can take the summer off and go fishing.

There are also the shallow creeks; two or three feet of gravel and lots of gold through it all, right from the top and way down into the bedrock. That's where you shovel everything into the boxes. But I am afraid that those shallow and rich creeks or gulches have all been found and mined out long ago. But still it's hard to tell what the man out in the field will run across.

Slate Creek, one of the placer mining camps on the

Upper Copper River drainage, was a good producer. The Slate Creek Mining Company had a big hydraulic pipe line, and a big crew of men were working for the company and getting big wages. The only fresh meat available in those days was what wild meat some of the men in the crew would shoot near the camp. The company paid them two bits a pound for it when they hunted on their off-time.

One evening two of the men, Miller and Kramer, went out looking for caribou. One of them carried a gun, and the other one carried a small shovel and a gold pan. Leaving Slate Creek, they climbed up through a narrow, steep gulch to a small tributary of Slate Creek with the intention of getting up on the high bench, a likely place for caribou. Once in a while they had to sit down and get their wind, it was that steep. About halfway up the gulch, there was a little pothole in the gravel, and it was full of water. Otherwise, the gulch was dry, as there had been a long dry spell. So they decided to wash a pan of gravel just for the fun of it. The gulch, they agreed, was almost standing on end, and it was impossible for any gold to have been deposited there. The first pan which they got right on the surface had about thirty-five cents' worth in it. They dug a little deeper and got two dollars and fifty cents. In a few minutes, they had panned out over thirty dollars.

They didn't go hunting. They quit their job the next morning, went back up the gulch, measured its length, and stepped it off. It was just one-half mile long; one claim for each.

They drew straws to see who would get the lower claim. Miller got it. Kramer got the upper claim. Then they staked the gulch. The company foreman laughed at them. Nobody could believe there would be any pay to speak of on a small gulch that steep. But what a gulch that was! The lower and upper claims turned out to be equal. One million dollars came off each claim. The company quit laughing when Miller and Kramer hired a big part of its crew and paid them twelve dollars a day instead of the seven or eight dollars the company was paying. After they had staked it and were ready to do some work, a steady rain set in, and in a short time they had bought lumber, made boxes, and had men shoveling into the boxes and making money faster than they had ever thought possible. Within a few years, Miller and Kramer left Slate Creek with over eight hundred thousand dollars to the good. Each of them, that is!

It was named Miller Gulch, and it was restaked and worked over again several times, and at least another million was taken out of there. This was one of the sweet short gulches that was shoveled into the sluice boxes by hand— every bit of it. It was so rich in places that they had to clean up several times a day, or the riffles would fill up with gold, and when that happened, the gold, or at least a big part of it, would wash out of the end of the box with the gravel. You could mine a gulch like that now in two years with a good big 'dozer. But I hate to think about the income tax you would have to pay.

It's not likely that anyone will stumble onto something like that now. But the seemingly impossible happens once in a while. It was impossible for Miller Gulch to have gold in it, too, as steep as it was. Still, it dished out over three million dollars, a good part of it worked out by hand.

Of course, we have the big companies with their draglines and dredges and all kinds of big heavy equipment. They are nice to have around, too. But if a prospector happens to find something too big for him to handle, he knows he can always sell it to them.

CHAPTER EIGHT

PAY DIRT

In the afternoon of May 13, 1913, a cold breeze and a drizzly rain was sweeping down what was soon to be known as Bonanza Creek, near the headwaters of the Chisana River in Alaska. At the mouth of the creek, three men had a big campfire going, cooking tea and having lunch. They were William James, Nels Peter Nelson, and Indian Joe. James and Nelson had come from Dawson in the Canadian Yukon Territory to the headwaters of the White River (on the Alaska side of the line) to prospect for copper deposits. They also had a sharp eye for any valuable minerals, such as placer gold.

They had been on the White the previous fall. It was there they had met Indian Joe when he was on his way back to his home on the Chisana River after a visit with some Canadian Indians. They were both experienced placer miners and prospectors, and they asked Indian Joe if he knew of any place where they could find copper or gold.

Joe said, "Well, I know one place. Big hill, funny looking rock." And he explained to them about a big, yellow dike. He told them it was about 50 miles from where they were on the White.

But it was too late to make the trip that fall. They had to get back to Dawson, a distance of 150 miles, before the snow caught them. Joe promised to meet them on the White River the next spring, and, true to his word, he was there waiting to guide them to the yellow dike. That was how the three men came to be around the big campfire on that cold, wet day.

Luck had been against James and Nelson the last three or four years. They were each nearly five thousand dollars in debt, which was almost a fortune at that time. They were beginning to wonder if their kind of life was worthwhile. They planned on building a new cabin in the Fortymile River country on the American side, that coming fall, where there were lots of moose. With a cache full of fat moose meat, it wouldn't cost much to live through the winter.

They stood there tired, wet and cold, bending over the flames, trying to get their clothes dry. They could not possibly know then that instead of cutting wood and eating moose meat next winter, they would be living in the best hotel in San Francisco, having an awful time learning how to order and eat meals in a high class dining room.

When they had satisfied their hunger, and their clothes were partly dry, it was agreed that Nelson and Joe would make some sort of a shelter for the night and cut some wood. James climbed up the hillside to bring down some samples of the yellow dike, which was located right there at the mouth of the stream they were on.

James was well schooled on hard rock, and he spent

quite a long time on the hillside. It was a big, wide, sulfur stained dike, and he wanted to examine it all the way across.

When Nelson and Joe got through putting a small canvas roof on some leaning poles, and making a windbreak with spruce boughs, Nelson let Joe cut the wood (they had only one axe) and took a shovel, pick and gold pan, and walked up stream about a quarter of a mile. There was a low bench, or gravel bar, on the left limit of the stream. It was a natural place to take a pan. The bedrock was about three feet above the water, and covered with about three feet of stream gravel. In other words, it was the old stream bed, left high and dry.

After shoveling off some gravel, he got his first pan right on bedrock, and it had about a dollar's worth of gold in it. When he saw the result, he looked up the hillside to where James was still picking away and breaking rocks, and he let out a war whoop as loud as he could, trying to draw James's attention. James didn't hear him but he happened to look down and he saw Nelson throw his hat up in the air, pick it up and throw it again. Then he threw the gold pan up, and caught it as it came down.

James came down to the camp where Joe kept the fire going, and had another cup of tea. By the time James and Joe got up to him, Nelson had over half an ounce of gold lying on a flat rock, and this was the mouth of the creek. Holy cats! What would it be farther upstream?

They named it Bonanza Creek, and the next few days they were busy staking claims. Indian Joe got the first claim named "Discovery." Upstream two and a half miles was a small tributary, the rich baby, shallow ground and lots of gold. They named it "Little Eldorado. Nineteen hundred and thirteen was the year that James and Nelson changed their luck!

23

James went with Indian Joe to the village where Joe was the Chief, about fifteen miles from the mouth of Bonanza. It was his plan to try and get some of the young, husky Indians to whipsaw some lumber for sluice boxes. They had whipsaws in the village, but luck hit again.

Bonanza Creek flows into what is now known as Johnson Creek, which, in turn, flows into the Chisana River. Following Johnson Creek down towards the river, they crossed a small stream about three miles below Bonanza. There they found that somebody had tried sluicing a few years before. But it evidently didn't pay, as they had left and didn't come back. There were lots of good sluice boxes, shovels, picks, a whipsaw, and a lot of other tools. So James hired a bunch of the young native boys to pack the boxes up to the little Eldorado.

In the meantime, Nelson had gone back to Dawson to get canvas, lead, and hose, and hire a bunch of men to shovel into the boxes. He also hired a man with a string of pack horses to bring in all the gear.

They had staked all the claims the law allowed, and of course, when Nelson came back from Dawson, the stampede was on. For the next two or three years, thousands of men came from all directions, but about the only pay dirt worthwhile was right along Bonanza Creek, and it never got to be a big camp like Dawson, or what is better known as the Klondike.

Nobody knows, and most likely never will know, how much gold they took out in the short time they mined that first summer. There was no red tape to bother with in those days. They took off to San Francisco that fall, stopping first at Cordova, where they deposited the gold in the bank, wrote out checks amounting to almost $10,000 to pay off

24

their debts, and then boarded the first steamboat to Seattle.

I got well acquainted with both of them some years later, especially Nelson, who lived to be almost a hundred. I worked for him in Chisana on a high bench on No. 5 on Bonanza in the 1930's, where he was still mining. I often tried to find out how much they took out that first summer, but all he would ever say was: "Well, if I told you, I doubt that you would believe it. And if you did, you would most likely ask me what the hell did you do with all the money? It was really a lot of fun," he said, "and believe me, we had some high class dinners out there in San Francisco. But I never did feel at home in them big, classy dining rooms. Regardless of how classy and good the food was, and wearing the fancy clothes, I always felt out of place. Many times when I was eating, I thought about the cabin we intended to build on the bank of the Fortymile River, and either coming home from a trip on snowshoes, or coming out of a prospect hole after digging all day, hungry as a wolf, and coming into a nice warm cabin with the old dutch oven plumb full of fat moose meat."

I said, "You must be kidding. Do you mean to tell me that you would rather sit in a little old cabin up here in Alaska, eating moose meat, than to have dinner out there in one of those first class eating places on the Pacific Coast?"

"Well, " he said, "here is the way I feel about it. I am a big man, but when I get out there in one of them big, classy dining rooms, I don't feel big at all. In fact, I feel small, and when I look at that great big hotel. I realize that I am small. But when I come home to my log cagin here on Bonanza, or downtown Chisana, that's my cabin, and regardless of whether I am rich, poor, big, or little, I feel big. And, by God, I am big!"

CHAPTER NINE

BILL CREATON

I met Bill Creaton in 1926. We both worked in the same camp for the Alaska Road Commission. Bill was 80 years old at the time, but in much better condition than most men at 50. He was an exceptional man, 6 feet 3 inches tall, powerfully built, healthy, strong, and as active as a man of 40. He was born in Austria, and came to the U.S. when he was 18 years old. He came to Alaska in 1886, and he never left. Sometimes he mentioned that when the time came for him to go through that unknown pass, he would settle right down in the permafrost.

I learned a lot about Alaska from Bill. We took a liking to each other as soon as we met and felt as father and son toward each other. He had spent 40 years in the hills, mining, prospecting and trapping, and anything I wanted to know about, I could always find out from him.

One day I said to Bill, "I'll bet you're getting tired of answering all my questions."

"Oh, no," he said. "No, not at all, son. I am always

26

glad to give any information I can to anyone who takes a liking to this far north country. I sort of feel towards you, Knut, as if you were my own boy. I know there is a lot more you want to ask me. You'll be in Alaska a long time, and there are lots of things thay you should know. You'll most likely be in the hills a big part of your life, like I have been, and it's a good life. After you have been in the hills awhile, you'll get a friendly feeling towards nature in general, toward the hills, streams, the woods, birds and all the wild life out there. I am not the handiest man in the world with a pen or pencil, but I am going to spend part of my evenings writing down just what it will be like for you out there in the hills. What I write down goes for you, or anyone else who may decide to break away from the old slave boat and find a world of their own to live in. I am not a fortune teller, but I'll bet you, son, that some day, many years from now, you'll say to yourself, 'By golly, old Dad Creaton was right'." And how right he was.

I had a hard time reading his handwriting, but managed to copy it off. I had it with me for many years in the hills, and I read it so often that I knew it by heart. Only when I sit and think of the many years I spent in the hills, I'll sort of whisper, "You *must* have been a fortune teller, Bill."

Once Bill actually retired and lived in a cabin along the Kenney Lake on the Chitina Road. Then he got restless, and went to work for the road commission in the summer of 1926, and that was where I met him. "I don't need to work," he said, "but I am feeling too good to sit around doing nothing."

The winter of 1926 and 1927, he trapped and did real well. When he wrote to me he always ended his letters with: "If you need any money, son, be sure to let me know."

27

In 1929 he sold his cabin and left. He sent me a card, saying he would let me know where he was at, as soon as he decided where to settle down and build a new cabin. The last I heard from him he was on the Koskikwim River. I answered his letter, but I never heard from him again. He may have written, but the mail wasn't too dependable in those days. I heard later that Bill was way past a hundred when he died.

Here is the outline he wrote for me:

You are interested in finding gold, son, and I don't blame you. It's a mighty fascinating game. It's a hard life, hard work, and a slim chance of finding anything worthwhile. But you'll be out there looking for it. You'll be digging and working like a lunatic because you are healthy, strong, and active. You'll be disappointed many times but it will only make you more determined than ever.

Study all the literature you can get on prospecting, mining and the rock formation. You'll have lots of time for it and it will help you a lot. You'll most likely pull out of the hills once in awhile and tell yourself that you have had enough of it, that you'll go to work somewhere and to hell with this idea of spending your life out here in these big wide open lonely places. At the same time you'll know damn well that you are lying to yourself.

You'll go to work on some job for awhile, but you'll soon get so damn lonesome for those lonely hills that before you know it, you are back out there, happy as a kid going to a circus.

Of course, if you find something worthwhile, you'll set up to mine it. I am sure you'll find that it's a lot more fun to prospect than it is to mine. A prospector is an explorer at heart. He has a strong urge to search for the unknown.

And remember, son, fur prices are high! You don't have to work for anybody. If possible, try and get a good partner and you'll find a world of your own out in them there hills. Unless you decide to go find yourself a wife, you'll find that the freedom you hear so much about is right out there in the hills waiting for somebody to go ahead and make use of it.

You'll be coming out to tangle with the girls once in awhile, maybe the natives and maybe the sporting girls. But unless you fall in love with some of them, you'll be back out in the hills telling yourself, 'By God, it's nice to be back here again. I am staying here now, and to hell with all the bright lights and the so-called modern way of life.'

These cycles will go on and on for years. You'll finally realize that regardless of what you tell yourself, you always come back into the hills when you lose interest in everything else. Whether it's under a big spruce tree, or tent or cabin, you'll feel at home. You become part of the wilderness. What really counts, son, is that you are enjoying life. And money or no money, what else could we wish for? Or what else is there?

So spoke William Creaton in 1926, and now fifty

29

years later I would like to add some more.

To Whom It May Concern:
Keep in mind that what you have just read happened way back in the 1920's and 1930's. Here
is what I want to add to it at this day and age:
As I have already mentioned, Alaska is no longer
free and open.

CHAPTER TEN

THE OLD OLD-TIMERS
AND THE NEW OLD-TIMERS

There will soon be an entirely new set of old-timers. The old dog and horse trail sourdough is almost out of existence. In fact, the new old-timers are already here. I've seen a few of them. I sat on a bar stool one hot July afternoon in 1963, having a cool bottle of beer, when a big man came in and sat down alongside of me and ordered a double shot of bourbon. "Can I buy you another drink?" he asked.

I said, "Okay, thank you. I'll have another beer."

He was already pretty high, and I kind of wondered why he ordered a double shot. He introduced himself, and I told him my name. He was a fast talker, and it was impossible to get a word in. I didn't care too much for his company, and I decided that as soon as I finished my drink, I would leave.

After telling me about all the things he could do and all the places he had worked, he said, "I am an old-timer in Alaska. I've been here since 1951."

I tried a couple of times to tell him when I came up

here, but he was like a wound-up phonograph—no chance to get a word in. I finally got up to leave, and said: "Thanks for the drink, I have to go."

I gave him some excuse, and just as I walked away from the bar, he asked, "When did you come to Alaska?"

I kept right on walking as I said, "Oh, I've been here quite a while." I knew the bartender, and he told me afterward that the big fellow asked him: "Who was that guy? Did you know him?"

The bartender said, "I'll say I know him, and I guess almost everybody does. That's the old sourdough that the grizzly bear tore all to hell in the fall of 1949."

The big man said, "Well, I'll be goddamn! Oh yes, I've heard about him. I wonder why he didn't tell me about it."

There's no denying that we've got them all here—the works! That means that there are bound to be a lot of good people—and there are. I believe that anyone who likes it well enough to settle down and make their home here is just the type this country neeeds. I've met a few of them. They usually stake a five-acre homesite along the highway, build a log house, raise a big garden, even if they have to haul topsoil from somewhere else. They take part-time jobs or whatever they can get, and they always seem to be happy and well satisfied just to have a place of their own. I've often heard them say, "Oh, well, this may be a long way from the modern way of life, but at least we own this place and no landlord is going to throw us out."

No rent to pay, no overhead to speak of, using wood for fuel in the winter and getting some wild meat in the fall. The head of the family usually gets a job some place nearby, at least for the summer months. And they are the type of people you can call old-timers. As soon as they settle down, they are here to stay!

Then there is another type, cursing the country and everything in it up and down. "Oh, what a hell of a country to be in. Why did I ever come to this godforsaken country?"

When they feel that way about it, they won't stay long. They'll get out somehow, either with their own car—if they have one—or they'll hitchhike a ride out of here.

In the old days there was no radio, no television, no telephone. At least, not out in the mining camps, except Fairbanks. Mail was a big event and the only entertainment. In some of the mining camps they got mail once a month, but in most of the smaller camps, no mail was delivered all summer so it was always eagerly received when it did come.

In one of the camps where I was mining, there were quite a few Indians. One Indian woman was married to an Eskimo who was working in another mining camp about a hundred miles from there. Once when she got a letter from her husband, she came to me and asked me to read it for her, as she couldn't read. The letter was well written. I forget just what it was all about, except one thing toward the end of the letter.

He wrote:

"I want you to make caribou skin parka with hood connection and also with fancy trimming at the bottom and wrist sleeves. Send it on August mail and be sure to charge plenty for it because this is for some white son-of-a-bitch who is part of the crew here."

When I finished reading the letter to her, she said, "I wish you write for me letter and I bawl him out plenty for

33

writing bad talk like that."

I said, "Okay, Clara, when do you want me to write your letter?"

She said, "Tomorrow I come over. I talk—you write."

And so she did. And this is part of the letter. I wrote down exactly what she dictated.

"Hello, Charlie, my husband,

First, I tell you I love you just the same. But goddamn you write like that to me. You talk white man for son-of-a-bitch. You know I like you. I like white man, too. But I sure don't like son-of-a-bitch! If you write nice letter, I make nice parka. I like to make nice parka for nice white man but I don't make parka for son-of-a-bitch. So don't look for parka on August mail and don't talk son-of-a-bitch in letter again. If you do I stop love for you. Because I can't read I have to get nice white man to read letter for me so you better remember no more son-of-a-bitch."

This was the main part of the bawling out. She didn't send him any parka on August mail, but she got another letter from him when the monthly mail came in. I came down to the winter quarters, or what we referred to as town, to get my mail, and once again I had to read her husband's letter to her. It was a nice letter. He told her that he was sorry about using bad words in his last letter. That he didn't really mean anything by it, and that it would be too late to make parka this year. It was a long letter about how lonesome he was without her, and all that sort of stuff.

The next day she dictated another letter and I wrote

34

it for her. Here it is in short:

"Hello, Charlie, my husband.
It make me feel like more love for you since you
learn to write nice letter. I soon get busy make
new parka for you because you need for hunting
this fall and you got lots of hunting to do. I
don't get many salmon in wheel and we need
lots food for dogs. I think good fox trapping this
winter. I see lots of fox pups and lots of birds
and rabbits."

She went on to tell him all the news. Charlie came home
that fall, and everything seemed to be okay. I kind of think
she broke Charlie of using bad names for nice white man.

CHAPTER ELEVEN

THE ODD BALLS

The Alaskan sourdoughs and last frontiersmen may not all be odd balls, but I am sure a lot of us are. Or, at least, they call us odd balls. I've overheard it at times concerning myself. Something like this, "Oh, he is a hell of a nice guy, but he is kind of an odd ball. When everybody else is watching TV, he'll be in another room by himself lost in a book. He won't go to a movie and a lot of other things. He'll join anybody having a few drinks, and let somebody start talking about a trip into the hills, and he'll really come to life. You can see the light shining right out of his eyes like two little light bulbs."

Well, I don't mind being called an odd ball. It seems every one of us has some sort of assignment to carry out in this short life span of ours. Whatever that happens to be, if we don't stumble onto it, I think a lot of us may be confused.

Not counting the professional tramp, bum, or criminal, there has always been a small percentage who deserted from the rat race of civilization to find their own kind of freedom. They were their own responsibility, and had no one to depend on except themselves. But to them it was lots more fun than to bow to the masters. Come what will, they had found something they would never let go of. Status, rank, or prestige had no meaning to them. They wanted to live this short span of life doing exactly what they wanted to.

In my days in Alaska, I've known many an odd ball. In general, he is a good man who can do almost anything. He has been offered many well paying jobs but working for wages is only an emergency with him. When he needs money he'll work for awhile, but during the time he is working he feels like a prisoner. As far as he is concerned, it would have been as well if the clock had never been invented. When on his own he goes to work any hour of the day or night, eats when hungry, rests when tired. When on a job he is conscientious about his work, but regardless of his skill in any kind of work, he has no intention of making a career or lifetime job of it. He may walk off the job any day without notice. So he'd be known as a good man but one who can't be depended on.

His true nature, whether he knows it or not, is to search for the unknown. He doesn't look down on anybody, regardless of caste, race or color. Neither does he look up to anyone, no matter how high he may have climbed. He is a sort of loner, although he is not necessarily lonesome. The herd instinct doesn't apply to his nature. Above all, he is a free agent.

Whatever he happens to take an interest in, he'll work hard at it. If it doesn't turn out like he thought it would, he won't cry about it. He doesn't pride himself on setting an example for the rest of humanity on how to live in this world. He is well aware that he is choosing a way of life for himself, and not for the rest of the world to copy.

Finally, the odd ball is not the type who wants to be noted. He has a tendency to avoid the crowd, and he may at times be branded unsociable, but such is not the case. Like anybody else, he needs company but he wants to choose his own.

A prospector may be contented and happy a hundred miles away from any place or anbody, in a little flimsy tent, working like a horse and singing all day long. Meanwhile a rich businessman living in a million dollar home may be so dissatisfied with life, that he picks up a gun and blows his brains out.

Stampeders from the gold rush days were odd balls. They came from all professions. Some of them turned out to be, or rather discovered that they were, prospectors. They put in the rest of their life at it. Money or no money, they had found the kind of life that they had no intention of quitting. And the happiest part of their life was the time they put in searching for the unknown.

A lot of others got out of the hills for good, and decided it was not the life for them. I guess it takes all kinds of us odd balls to make a world.

CHAPTER TWELVE

ALASKA INDIANS

I got well acquainted with a lot of the Indians on the Upper Copper River and the Upper Tanana River. I soon noticed that here was a race of people in the wilderness living a free life. Nobody tried to outdo anyone else or dominate each other. Nobody worried about getting ahead in this world. Nobody was concerned about what might happen tomorrow, next day, next month, next year, or ten years from now. Do what must be done today, they believed.

They helped each other when necessary and were a jolly, social, and friendly race of people scattered throughout Alaska in small and big villages. They were good hunters, trappers and fishermen. Their main purpose in life? To be free. To do as they pleased, and make today the most important day of all.

They loved and enjoyed their way of life. But alas! It was soon to be changed, supposedly for the better. But I doubt that they'll ever be as happy and free as they were.

One day I had a long talk with one of the chiefs,

Chief Long. He was very bright, and could speak fairly good English. I asked him if he was boss in the village.

He said, "Yes, and no. Everybody is free to live their own way. That's our main aim in life. But in case of dispute we must have a chief and other officers. It's very seldom that we have any trouble, but when we do, we decide who is right and who is wrong, and our decision is always respected. Then, if any of the parties concerned wish to move to some other village, arrangements will be made for them to do so.

"We all like to hunt and fish. We help each other to dry cure meat and fish, and gather other food, like peavine roots and berries, to be stored for winter. The chief don't sit on a high seat with a crown on his head and look wise. He helps with everything like all the rest. We visit each other a lot, and have much fun. We go visit other villages when we can, and they come see us too. Everybody loves the children, and helps raise them and learn them how to do things. When meat is scarce, everybody hunt. If one gets meat, we all have meat, and then we keep hunting until we feel we can relax again.

"Quite often we have to move camp to where the game is more plentiful. If we get seriously short on meat, we always know where we can go and get fish, and as a rule, we have a lot of dried meat and fish stored away for emergency. So we don't worry. We are usually too busy living today to be concerned about tomorrow. We have no strict rules or laws, as there is no need for it.

"We live in villages and hunting camps, and everybody is eager to contribute all they can towards keeping the village supplied. We don't have any money, and yet nobody is broke because the whole village is our bank. We are all

40

shareholders. Trapping season we scatter in all directions, and most of the women and older people look after the village, and take care of the children. Well, my friend, we had a long visit. I have to go now. I see you sometime."

I thanked him, and after he left, I wrote down what he had been telling me. This was more of a free life than anything I had ever seen anywhere. Everybody seemed to be well contented, healthy and strong. Cabins, tents, wood, meat, fish, and fur were their main concern. They respected each other as equals. Nobody tried to keep up, or get ahead of anyone else. There was no sign of greed. A village was more like a big family. If one of the men decided to go hunting, he just let the village know about where he intended to hunt, so that in case he didn't come back within a reasonable length of time, a search would be made for him.

If he got a moose, he would bring home the liver, explain where the meat could be found, and soon a big bunch of men, women, boys, girls, and a few dogs, would be on their way to take care of the meat and bring it home.

During the 1920's, and most of the 1930's, the natives made good money on fur, and fairly good from then until almost 1950. But after that, the prices dropped and dropped. It would be hopeless for a native today to even think of supporting his family by trapping and hunting. The game laws forbid him to kill meat out of season. Besides that, Alaska is now overcrowded with big game guides, so the hunting ground has been turned over to the sportsmen. The days of the Alaskan Indians' wilderness freedom have long since come to an end.

CHAPTER THIRTEEN

HOW DUMB? HOW SMART!

Lido Nicholie was an Indian chief on the Upper Copper River. His main headquarters was at the mouth of a stream called Indian River, a tributary of the Copper. I first met him when I worked for the Alaska Road Commission in 1928. The road caught up with his camp that summer. One of the men of our crew asked Nicholie a lot of questions, but the chief didn't understand English too well. Most of his answers were: "No savvy."

After the man got tired of asking questions, he came into our tent.

"I wonder how dumb they can get," he growled.

"He is the chief over all the Indians on the Upper Copper River," I said, "and I've got a hunch he may be plenty smart in his own way."

I was to find out a couple of years later how true that was.

When the road work shut down that fall, my brother and I built a cabin at Indian River, which was the end of the road at that time. We did some trapping and prospecting, and I got well acquainted with the old chief, and I liked him real well. He was an old man. I think he was about seventy-five. He wore his hair long, was about six feet tall, and was straight as a soldier on parade. He had learned to talk better English, and we could talk about anything. We used sign language if we had to. I learned a lot about the outdoors from him.

During the winter of 1930, I learned something that gave me a surprise. There were a lot of caribou around that winter, and the old Chief was the meatgetter in the village, because the younger men were too busy chasing around from one village to the next and getting drunk when they could get the booze. The Chief didn't drink, and he was against all intoxicants.

One day he told me that he was going across the Copper River to kill some caribou.

"Tomorrow, me come back," he said.

That night it turned real cold. The next day at eleven a.m., it was forty-eight below zero. I thought to myself, oh boy, this must have been a bad night for camping out. I was worried about him, so I put on lots of clothes and walked down to the river bank to look across. I saw that there was heavy overflow water on top of the ice. Almost all the rivers in Alaska overflow every few days in the winter, and lots of feet have been frozen on account of it.

I didn't see any smoke on the other side and I was about to turn back and go home, when I saw a man coming out of the woods across the river. I looked through my field glasses, and sure enough, there was the Chief. I could see him through the glasses as if he were right in front of me. He looked up and down the stream. Because of the cold, there was a layer of fog evaporating from the open water. There seemed to be no end to the overflow either way. I saw him shaking his head, and I thought he was going back to where he came from. Then he walked back toward the woods. He made a slight turn to the left upstream, and made a beeline for a dry spruce tree with a lot of boughs on it. When I saw him breaking off a bunch of dry boughs and stacking them up in a neat little bundle, I began to wonder what he was up to. Perhaps he was getting cold and had to get a fire going. Moreover, the chances were he had gotten his feet wet and had to dry his moccasins.

I was getting cold myself. I had to jump around and run back and forth to keep warm. But I couldn't leave. He had me puzzled, and I had to see the outcome of this. I didn't want to build a fire, as I didn't want the chief to know I was watching him. Then I saw him pulling a thin piece of rope out of his parka pocket. He tied it around his little bundle of spruce boughs. He also picked off two pieces of bark from the trunk of the tree and hung his gun in the same tree. Next, he walked back to the edge of the water again. He laid the spruce boughs and bark on the ice, took off his parka, sat down on it, and took off his moccasins and socks. He rolled his pants legs and underwear up above his knees. Next he stepped off the parka onto a piece of bark. He picked up the spruce boughs and put them in the crook of his left arm, placed his socks and moccasins on the top of the bundle, and put his parka over the whole batch.

Then he laid the other piece of bark ahead of him, close to the water. He stepped on it with his right foot. The next step, with his left foot, hit the water. Once in the water, he walked fairly fast. Every time he moved his foot ahead, he pointed the toes downward to keep from splashing. At times, the water came almost to his knees, but he came across in a few minutes. When he got to the edge of the water again, he kept his feet in the water. He threw the parka ahead of him onto the dry ice. Then he jumped on the parka and sort of pulled it around his feet. He laid the bundle of dry spruce on the ice and lit it with a match. He swung his feet in and out of the long, hot flames, and rubbed them with a scarf that he took off his neck. He sat down on the parka, put on his socks and moccasins. He stepped off the parka, picked it up, shook it, and put it on.

He took off on the run for the woods where I was hiding. That was all I saw. I was cold and shivering, but I had witnessed the impossible. No man could cross all that water wearing only moose-hide moccasins for footgear in forty-eight below zero, without freezing his feet. Still, there he was, coming on the run. He was dry as could be, and had a big smile on his face. I couldn't help but think of the man in the crew a couple of years before who had said, "How dumb can they get?"

I had learned something that was well worth knowing, something I never could have learned in school. Although I've never had to do it, I've always had the feeling that I know how to get across, if I have to—thanks to Chief Nicholie.

About a week after this incident, I questioned him one day.

"Say, Chief, how is the best way to get across a big river when there is overflow water on it and it is real cold weather?"

His answer was, "No go. No go. Much better no go. Maybe lose foot."

I knew he would have told me what to do, but he knew he would have a hard time explaining to me so I would understand. He just said, "No go." He didn't know that he had given me a real demonstration of how it could be done.

Now for a little explanation. Regardless of how cold it is, as long as your feet are in the water and you are moving, they won't freeze. If you step on dry ice with wet feet when it is forty or fifty below zero, you can't pull your feet off the ice. If you try, you will pull the skin off the bottoms of your feet. That was why the chief used the bark and the parka.

Not so dumb, after all!

CHAPTER FOURTEEN

NATURE IN ALASKA

We say that nature in the raw is seldom mild, which is true; that nature favors no man, which means that she operates under laws pertaining to particular circumstances; and that nature is always full of wonders.

If you and I meet on the trail and I am bucking a terrible head-on wind, you are almost being pushed along and about to apply the brake. The wind is neither bucking me nor favoring you. It is simply blowing like it is because certain conditions cause it to do so. There is nothing we can do to change it. The law governing it will eventually do that.

The law of gravity pulls the water back out to the ocean where it came from. Another law picks it up again, lifts it way up in the air, and sends it back in over the land where no life could exist without it.

So while it may be true that nature in the raw is seldom mild, we see that it is often good, besides being very interesting. We can also see how helpless we would be if it didn't work exactly as it does. But in this busy world we don't notice nature at work. We are too busy getting out of each other's way. But whether or not we notice her, she cares not a whit; still we instinctively know that we can depend on her. Nature is the biggest show in existence, and it's a lot of fun watching her. It appears to be a never-ending show, and we all have a lifetime ticket.

But there are so many things we take for granted, and therefore fail to notice. For instance, if the stars would be on display just one night each year, how many million people would be out of the house that night to watch the brilliant show in the blue sky overhead? But they are up there every night, and millions of people don't even look up. We are moving so fast on the highway and through the air now that we don't see anything. We may drive across the most beautiful stretch of country at 70 miles an hour, and all we see is more cars speeding along like ourselves. If we look, we'll see more in one hour's walking than we'll see in a day's riding. Of course it makes no difference how slowly we move; if we don't look we won't see anything.

Once I sat down to rest at the root of a big spruce tree, and I soon noticed there was a lot of activity in that tree. Right alongside of me were two little tunnels about half an inch apart. Between the two tunnels was a walkway about a quarter of an inch wide, and the big, black tree ants were hard at work. It was like watching a big fleet of dump trucks. There was a continuous string of ants coming out of one tunnel, loaded with sawdust. They dumped their load overboard, turned to the right onto the quarter inch walkway, and disappeared into the next tunnel on their way to another load. I had a big, wide magnifying glass, and I spent the rest of the day with them. I also camped under another spruce tree close by that night.

Directly above the two tunnels was a smaller tunnel, and every few minutes a big, black ant stuck his head out and watched the crew at work. He was most likely the superintendent, or some sort of boss. Once I held the magnifying glass almost against him, and at the same time laughed out loud. It didn't faze him a bit.

I was tired, as I had been carrying a heavily loaded packboard all day. So I rested there till noon the next day. If anybody had seen me leaving after saying good-bye to the ant settlement, and laughing as if someone had been telling a funny joke, they would most likely have said, "There is another guy going bushy!"

I've watched beavers through field glasses, felling trees, carrying mud and rocks, and building dams. I've watched them sitting on their butts and turning the foot-long willow branches or twigs, shaving off the green bark with their sharp teeth. The way their fingers worked while turning the stick, you would almost swear they were playing a flute.

I've watched the mountain sheep feeding in the evening on the west side of the hill at sundown. Then they walk across the top of the ridge to lie down for the night on the east side, so that the rising sun will hit them in the morning.

There is a continuous show out there in the wilderness. All the wild life you see seems to be so well contented it brings to mind Walt Whitman's *Leaves of Grass*, in which he tells how he gazed admiringly at animals who enjoy nature as it was intended for them.

I think I could turn and live with animals, they're so placid and self-contain'd,

I stand and look at them long and long.

49

They do not sweat and whine about their condition,

They do not lie awake in the dark and weep for their sins,

They do not make me sick discussing their duty to God,

Not one is dissatisfied, not one is demented with the mania of owning things,

Not one kneels to another, nor to his kind that lived thousands of years ago,

Not one is respectable or unhappy over the whole earth.

Throughout Alaska there are thousands of square miles of lonesome stretches that may seem dull and monotonous, but if we really look, we usually find many places where nature is putting on a show of some kind. In most cases we are, or rather think we are, too busy to spend any time watching it. But regardless of how lonely and monotonous the trail seems to be, as you walk along, mile after mile, you'll notice there are a couple of camp robins along with you, always landing in a tree a few feet ahead of you. They know you are going to have a lunch sometime. And even if you don't give them anything, they know you"ll spill a few crumbs. You may not see them at first, but they will be your constant companions as you hike along, so look up and enjoy them.

CHAPTER FIFTEEN

ABOUT THE ROADS

It amuses me when I hear complaints about the roads in Alaska. I hear it continuously, especially in the summertime when there are a lot of strangers up here. I hear them talk in the bars, restaurants, lobbies and motels. "Oh, what a horrible road! How can they have nerve enough to call it a road! In places, it almost throws you through the top of the car." But they forget to mention that in most cases the warning sign will say slow to thirty-five miles per hour, but they'll hold their speed to sixty, seventy, and eighty.

I've often been asked about road conditions, and I usually tell them that if they'll watch for all the signs along the road, and do what the signs tell them to, they'll be okay. I never argue with them about the roads when they insist that the Alaskan roads are man-killers. It's a whole lot easier just to act dumb, and at the same time have a little laugh to myself, thinking back to the days when I came through with dog teams or pack horses, and sometimes afoot with a heavy pack on my back. We used to be well satisfied if we made from twenty to thirty miles in a day. But now some of the people who come up here just to see the country will curse and condemn the whole region if they can't make from five to seven or eight hundred miles a day. Just take it easy, boys and girls, ladies and gentlemen. If you came up here to see the country, you surely won't see much of it at that rate of speed. A race track would be a much better place for you to go than the bumpy, winding roads in Alaska. If you came up here to see how fast you can see Alaska, your eyes will be glued to the road, and you won't see anything.

If you happen to be one of those people who hate to see a car pass you, don't let it bother you here. Just let them pass. Most likely you'll catch up with some of them either in the ditch, over the bank, or hooked on behind some wrecker or tow truck.

Most of the tourists who come up here in their own cars are so busy trying to fulfill the program they have laid out for themselves, that they can only spend so much time here and so much there. Their main objective is to see how many miles they can make in a day. I've heard so many of them say: "We want to see Fairbanks, Anchorage, Valdez, and fly over to Kodiak and also Nome and the Arctic Circle. And we only have so much time."

I believe it would be much better if you didn't have any program at all, but spent as much time as you felt like at anything you enjoy. And if you see only part of Alaska this year and take time to enjoy it, come on up and see the rest of it next year, or whenever you can. If you take your time to enjoy it, you'll come back.

CHAPTER SIXTEEN

THE GOOD OLD DAYS

It always seems to me like there are two Alaskas—the old and the new. And they are as different as night and day. I never seem to be able to get in the habit of locking my door, and I really don't think that my place is any safer when it's locked up. I can't recall ever having lost anything when I left the door unlocked, I kind of think that if your place is unlocked and if anyone is planning on busting in to steal anything from you, they'll feel uneasy if they find the place unlocked. They'll think that you are right close by, or you would have locked the door.

In old Alaska, nobody ever thought of locking their doors except right in town, and even there a lot of them didn't bother to lock their place if they went away for a while. Out in the hills it was considered almost an insult to lock your door. Any cabin, house, tent or any sort of camp was your home to use as long as you needed it, and if you took anything, you left a note telling what you had been using.

You usually found most places in good condition, and before you left, you made sure it was in as good shape as you had found it, leaving more wood cut than you had burned. And in those days when you had been away from your place for any length of time, you always kind of hoped that someone had been there while you were away. It was natural to hope to find a note from somebody, and maybe a bit of news at the same time. But now it's quite different. If you've been away for a while now, and you are on your way back home, you hope that nobody has been around your place—and for a good reason. You may find everything okay, but on the other hand, you may find that somebody has broken in and stolen God knows what, and made a hell of a mess out of everything in the house.

I'll give you a few examples of the way things often happened in Old Alaska.

Once I went with a couple of friends on a four-day fishing trip. After we got out to where we made camp, I discovered that I had left my wallet containing more than $100 in a pair of pants hanging on the wall of my cabin. And the door wasn't locked. In fact, I didn't have a lock for it. I didn't worry about it and the money was still there when I came back.

Once in a mining camp, I came from the Post Office and brought mail for several of the miners along the creek. In one of the camps, there was no one at home and on the table was a big gold scale with about two thousand dollars on it, and some in a bowl alongside of it. I left his mail right on top of the gold, and then I wrote a note telling him that next time I would bring my poke along and if there was any gold on his scale, I would collect for being his mail carrier.

One fall, or early winter, there was a bunch of miners

54

from Chisana, a small placer mining camp, traveling together across the Chisana Glacier with several teams of dogs. They were headed for McCarty, a small town along the Copper River Railroad, where they bought their supplies. It was fifty-two miles across the glacier, so they had to put up overnight in small tents. They used both kerosene stoves and wood stoves, as they usually had a cache of wood on the hillside along the slope of the glacier.

As everybody was busy getting all set for the night, one Dud McKinny started in to make an awful racket, swearing and cursing.

"Where the hell is my bag of beans?" he demanded.

The rest of the bunch asked him, "What's the matter, Dud?"

"I can't find my bag of beans."

"Oh, forget it, Dud. We got lots of beans. You can have all you want."

But Dud McKinny said, "No, goddamn it. I want my own beans."

When he finally did find the can, they saw the reason why he wanted his own beans. He opened the bean bag and pulled out a poke with about $6,000 in it. He wasn't worried about anybody stealing it, but he thought it was a good place to have it, to keep from losing it.

You may have read about the old Alaska gold miners, how they carried six-shooters, and what a tough bunch of roughnecks they were. They were tough—you bet your life they had to be. At times they had to sleep out under the spruce trees in any kind of weather, and sometimes under the open sky, be it cloudy, raining, snowing, or crystal clear. They had to fight the elements to get their supplies into the mining ground, and it was no job for a weakling. There were no gunslingers or man killers among them. They were an average bunch of honest, hard-working, strong and healthy men, and what little trouble they did have among themselves was more like a big family squabble.

It's easy to see that in a country like this, before there were any roads, airplanes and fields, it was too uncomfortable for thieves, crooks, pimps, or any of the fancy professions. Of course, there were usually some sporting women wherever any amount of money came out of the ground, but in some ways they seemed to be much like the miners. They wouldn't gyp a man out of his hard-earned money. In fact, some of them often helped the miners out if they needed a bit of cash. Some of them made good money by grubstaking prospectors to go out and search for new diggings.

The old Alaskans always referred to them as the girls, and they didn't like it at all to hear anybody calling them whores. All I want to say about them is that life would have been too dull without them. I met one in Seattle once. I knew her real well. Her name doesn't matter here. I was broke and I wanted to get back to Alaska—the quicker the better. I didn't want her to know that I was broke, and I told her I had a way figured to get back. But it didn't take her long to find out that I was broke and she asked me: "How much do you need, Knut?"

I said, "How did you know I was busted?"

"Oh," she said, "that's easy. As well as I know you, I know that you would have asked me to go with you either to dinner, a show, or anything."

I said, "Okay, sweetheart, if you can spare a hundred dollars, I'll be on that boat leaving tomorrow afternoon."

She handed me five twenties, took me out for dinner, and I spent the night with her in her apartment. She didn't lose anything by it. That was one of the girls from old Alaska, and that was about the way we got along with them. You don't find that kind anymore, and, of course, they couldn't be that way now even if they wanted to. The people in Alaska now are no longer an average lot. All kinds—and I mean *all* kinds—are here now. The works!

CHAPTER SEVENTEEN

LOOK OUT FOR GRIZZLY BEARS

When Ole Haugland went out to use his air-cooled engine to sharpen tools that morning, he didn't realize what a shock he would soon experience. Ole was a sixty-year-old prospector, and owned a cabin near Slana, Alaska. He was anxious to get some work done, since it was almost noon.

When I approached him, I was afraid he would faint at the sight of me. I made some guttural sounds to attract his attention. Ole was hard of hearing. I grunted again. This time louder. Ole finally looked up from his noisy engine. Shock and disbelief were in his eyes. I thought he would fall over in a faint. Small wonder. I had been the victim of a grizzly bear's attack.

He stood there in a daze, unable to move. Finally, after a long silence, he said, "Oh, Christ! Knut, what happened? A bear?"

I could only nod my head, meaning: "Yes." I experienced a sad feeling when I realized that I could not talk.

A few minutes before this, I had tangled with the

most vicious grizzly bear in Alaska. It had attacked me from out of nowhere. My scalp was partly torn off, my face gnawed in half, my wrist clawed savagely, and my thigh was chewed up like a hamburger.

I pointed at the cabin door, indicating that I wanted to go in and lie down. I was, oh, so tired! Just let me lie down forever.

Ole got busy. He stopped the little motor and got me into the cabin. I lay down on a mattress on the floor.

Ole said, "I am going for help."

As he went out the door, I made a throaty noise, and pointed at his gun hanging at the doorway.

"That's right," he said. "I guess I better take it along today."

He left again and forgot to close the door. So I bellowed again and pointed at the door. He closed the door in a hurry. I heard him take off at a trot. He made good time for a man past sixty years old. He ran a mile, started his car, and drove four miles in seventeen minutes. I knew there was only one thing for Ole to do. That was exactly what he was doing—going for help. Still, I hated to see him leave.

I felt so lonesome after he had gone, but when I had rested a while I got up on my shaky legs again. I took a mirror off the the wall and looked at my face. That was a bad mistake! Now I could see why Ole almost fell backward. I almost did the same thing. But somehow I didn't panic. I knew one thing for sure. I was beyond repair. My time was up. Why had Ole left me? Nothing could be done anyway. I tried not to be concerned about it. At least, people knew now what had happened to me, and that seemed all that mattered.

I looked in the mirror once more, but I couldn't stand

it. There was no face there to look at. I guessed my romance with Lady Luck was over. I remembered all the times in the past she had rescued me.

One morning in the middle of November, 1923, I woke up in a cheap hotel in Seattle. I had a moonshine hangover, a terrible headache, and was weak and nervous. I had three dollars and eighty-five cents in my pocket.

I looked out the window, and it was pouring down buckets of rain. I sat on the bed and talked to myself. "Oh, well," I said, "there's no one but yourself to blame. I'm glad there is no one but you doing the suffering. I'll go over to the American Legion this afternoon and see if they know of work some place. There are so many strikes going on. The I. W. W. is on the warpath."

Two hours later I talked to a fellow in front of an employment agency. He told me that he was leaving for Alaska in about five days to work in the Kennecott Copper mines.

"They are hiring men," he said. "Why don't you come along?"

I went with him to their office, but they had their quota for that shipment of men on the old Victoria.

Anyway, my new friend was a good plug. He said, "Hell, I'll loan you the money to buy a steerage ticket and you can hire out in Cordova." He was right. He had been there before. So Lady Luck was still with me, as she had been through the Argonne Forest, the St. Mihiel, and Metz Front, when the earth seemed to be lifting all around us.

I liked it in Alaska. I worked in the Kennecott Mine that first winter. For the next few years I worked in many different places, and tried my hand at a lot of different things. I liked the people up here, and I made good money at times. I made trips back to the states, but I always returned to Alaska. I heard so much about prospecting and gold mining that I knew I would have to give it a try.

My brother came to Alaska in 1929, and we took off for the hills. We spent a number of years prospecting, doing some small-scale placer mining and trapping, and that was more fun than anything we had ever done.

But now here I was, lying on the floor of Ole's cabin, bleeding to death from a grizzly bear attack.

It began to get cold in the cabin. I couldn't keep warm, so I tried to build a fire in the stove. I put in some wood shavings and kindling, but no luck. I struck one match after another, but my hands and arms were bleeding so fast that it was hopeless to get a match to burn. While I was striking matches, I also tried to light a cigarette by placing it in the left side of my mouth. I tried to hold my torn-off face and upper lip in place with one hand. It was all doomed to fail, but it helped to keep me occupied. Then, before I even expected it, I heard voices and footsteps outside the cabin.

When Ole pulled into the road camp, the foreman, Clayton Hoy knew there was something wrong, because Ole almost rolled his pickup. The cook, Lillian Hoy, got busy on the telephone, and in a short time all the arrangements had been made. The news was spreading fast along the road. The Tenth Rescue Squad of the Army recognized the call, and indicated that they would come for me. The highway patrol agreed to stop all traffic as soon as I came out to the highway to be hauled the thirty miles from Slana to Chestochina.

When I think of it now, I sometimes wonder, "Who was I to rate all that consideration?" Even a fleet of road commission gravel trucks was ordered to stay off the road until I had passsed on the way to Chestochina. A grader had been sent ahead to smooth the rough spots while they were waiting for me to be brought out to the road. All this was being done for me while I lay on the cabin floor, thoroughly convinced that my world had come to an end.

When Ole came back with two husky men from the road crew, I had just finished making a sort of a will by tearing an old calendar off the wall. On the back side of it I scribbled: "Give my dogs and cabins and whatever I had to my brother, Ole, in Cordova." It was hard to read, as I had to write with my left hand. I was so happy to see Ole again. I held my lip in place with my hand and said to Ole, "You made good time."

They all got busy and picked me up, mattress and all, put me in Ole's boat, and took me down the river about four miles to where it ran parallel with the highway. The rest of the crew was there to help me get off the boat and up the bank. On the road, a new panel car was waiting for me. A nurse was there to be with me on the thirty-mile trip. There were a lot of strong and willing hands. They picked up the makeshift stretcher as though it were a bag of feathers. The nurse, Mrs. Cluff, and an engineer, Mr. Steffen, were in the panel with me. They both spoke to me and Mrs. Cluff held my bloody hand. I was in no condition to put up an argument.

What I really wanted was to be taken to my cabin and put into my own bed. I did manage to hold my lip in place and ask them, "Do you think it is worthwhile?" Of course they handed me a long line of sweet words. I still love them for it, but it just didn't make sense. I was getting weaker by the minute.

We made good time on the thirty-mile stretch. Clayton Hoy was driving. He knew that we wouldn't meet any cars, so he drove as fast as he dared to go.

When we arrived at the airport, we learned that the plane had arrived just five minutes ahead of us. Once more they picked me up, mattress and all. They put me on the ground close to the plane. The doctor came over and gave me a shot in the right arm, because the left one looked as if it were about to fall off. The muscle in the upper arm, close to the shoulder, had been bitten clear to the bone. It looked like it was trying to roll itself off my arm.

Then the doctor asked the group, "Do you have his scalp? If not, try to find it and bring it to the hospital at once." Later I learned that they found it and brought it in. But it was too late.

To get aboard I had to get off the mattress. By this time all the raw wounds began to ache terribly with pain. I did a lot of moaning and groaning before they got me seated. I'll never forget the expression on the pilot's face. He looked at me and turned his head away and shook it in a manner of disbelief. The doctor sat right next to me. I asked by signs for a drink of water. I was very thirsty.

"You'll soon feel better," he said. "We'll be in the hospital before long and then you'll get a drink."

How right he was! The shot he had given me made me feel better and better by the minute. In a few minutes I actually didn't think the whole thing amounted to a hell of a lot. I thought that in a couple or three days I would be right back in the woods to get some of those crazy bears.

We landed, and there were a lot of soldiers to help me from the plane to the ambulance. It was another five or ten miles to the Air Force Hospital.

It had been a long, long, painful day. I had been

63

mauled at about eleven in the morning. It was now five in the evening. I was told later by the doctors and nurses that another hour would have ended my aches and pains forever.

Colonel Browning, who I had met previously, was in charge of this hospital. He had already gone to his living quarters, but was asked to come back because of this emergency. When he appeared, I was about to jump off the litter and shake hands with him. Of course he didn't recognize me. I tried to talk, but that didn't work very well. No one could understand me, but he could tell that I was trying to tell him something.

He went to the safe where they had already put my wallet. When he saw my name and address, he hurried back, looked at me, and said, "Yes, Knut, you do know me. Don't worry, we'll soon have you fixed up."

He had summoned all the surgeons and doctors that were available. I was getting sleepy and tired. I remember being wheeled in to the operating room. It seemed like a whole army was along with me.

They worked on me for hours to save my life. Soldiers donated blood. When they gave me ether, it was all guesswork. But everybody did the best they could and hoped for a miracle. My right thigh was so badly chewed that it looked almost hopeless. Part of it had to be discarded, as there was no way it could be put in place. The nurses told me that when cleaning my wounds, they found dirt, moss, pieces of underwear, leaves and spruce needles. The surgeons took turns sewing. When the job was done, no one knew how many stitches there were. But when they took them out, they counted four hundred and eighteen of them.

When I woke up in a private ward, it took me several moments to realize where I was, and what it was all about.

Colonel Browning was there, and he asked how I was feeling. My face and head seemed to be encased in a cement block. I couldn't say a word but I nodded my head to indicate that I was okay. I communicated with them by writing with my left hand.

A year or two before the accident, I had met Colonel Browning and his wife, Sally, at Slana while they were on leave. We took a great liking to each other. They enjoyed talking to old timers about mining, prospecting, trapping, hunting, fishing, and dog mushing. They liked my dog team. I told them all I knew about the wildreness. I stressed the point always to carry a gun if they went very far from the road. Once the Colonel had asked me if I always carried a gun when leaving the road. I said, "Yes, I do. You're never safe without one." He assured me that he would take my advice.

The sad part of all this was my negelect of my own advice. Colonel Browning saved his remarks till I recuperated. Right now I was just a bundle of nothing.

I was in that ward about ninety days, and while I had to go through a lot of suffering, they all treated me like a long-lost brother. They actually made me feel like I wanted to live. The worst part of all the suffering I went through was a headache that lasted four months. It was so intense and painful that I was given a couple of painkillers every four hours. They would relieve the pain for two hours. So I spent half the time suffering and waiting for my two capsules. Then after four months, the headaches gradually went away. What a relief that was! Afterward, I began to gain back some of the weight I had lost. In a year I was somewhat normal. But after a deal like that, I could never expect to be the same again.

They finally let me go home to Slana for a while. My neighbor's wife, Mrs. Bronnicke, took care of my scalp. The bandage had to be changed every day. It took two and a half years for it to grow over the bare skull. It built a thin layer of flesh. On its surface is a very thin layer of scar tissue which is always giving me some trouble. It is so thin and tender that any little thing that happens to hit it, ever so lightly, will break it. It is always slow to heal.

The bone specialist didn't think my right wrist would ever be any good. The other doctors didn't think my left arm would be any good, because the muscle on the upper arm had been cut completely in two, clear to the bone. Miraculously, both my wrist and arm regained their normal functions. My right leg was a little weak for three or four years, but it gradually got stronger.

I started thanking Lady Luck again, as I had done so many times in the past. She always seemed to appear just in time. Like she has been doing ever since I left Denmark in 1914, and came to the United States. She never put a handful of diamonds in my pocket, but I got so I depended on her when things began to look hopeless. She never did fail me—she never will!

Colonel Browning and I kept in close touch, since he was the manager of the hospital. He kidded me in a friendly sort of way about leaving my 30.06 in my car. "Just when are you going to get around to telling us about what actually happened?" he chided me.

I promised him that I certainly would tell him. Indeed, I had much to say about Mr. Grizzly Bear, so the colonel sat down to listen to my filibuster on the subject.

66

CHAPTER EIGHTEEN

ROARING FURY

It was the last day of August, 1949, and almost the last day of Knut Peterson. I had spent a big part of my life prospecting, and at that time I owned a cabin and a five-acre homesite about seven miles north of Slana, and a mile east of the road on the bank of the Slana River.

A friend of mine by the name of Ole Haugland, who also was a prospector, owned a cabin on up the road. We had done some prospecting together, and the day before, I went up to see him about going with me on a prospecting trip up the big Tok River.

I left my old car at the road and walked the well-beaten trail to Ole's cabin. I stayed overnight, and we talked about gold and uranium, and all kinds of rich deposits. Ole had other plans, and he didn't want to go with me. So I decided to go alone.

I left Ole's cabin about eleven in the morning, to go back up to the road. I planned to get my car, go back to Slana, and get ready for the trip I had planned.

But I got only five hundred yards from his place when it happened. Talk about a surprise attack—it was like an earth-shaking thunder coming out of a sky without a cloud in it. A terrible roar erupted right back of me, and when I turned, there he was! A seven or eight-hundred-pound grizzly, charging full blast for all he was worth, straight at me at a fast gallop. He was roaring and snorting.

This was one of the few times that I was without my old 30.06. For a few seconds, I froze to the very spot on which I stood. When I was able to move, I thought of the Slana River just a few yards from the trail. I had tennis shoes on my feet, and when I did move, believe me, I moved fast. I was trying to make the bank of the river, dive into it and go with the current back to Ole's cabin. Just one more minute and I believe I would have made it.

I was running for all I was worth, my heart was pounding like a trip hammer, and all of a sudden I felt a big hairy paw on my left shoulder. Down I went, with a mad, roaring and snorting, frothing-at-the-mouth grizzly! He was hitting, biting, and tossing me around, and in a few seconds, I was all butchered up.

This is exactly what happened, and there were no witnesses—except me. Even now I feel like I want to pull down a curtain, and look the other way. When a person gets mauled as badly as I did, it's impossible to remember much about the actual beating. But I do remember part of it.

Once I was lying on my back. He came directly at my face with his big open mouth. I struck at his nose with my right hand and hollered, "Ole!" for all I was worth. He grabbed my right arm right at the wrist and I could feel the bones being crushed, but it saved my face that time. He finally got to it later. I wore a cast on that arm for the next six months. He bit into my right thigh, and put one of his paws right on my stomach, just above the pelvis. Again I hollered, "Ole!", with all my might.

I don't know why, but somehow I seemed to have the idea that Ole was close enough to hear me. I guess he was, but for one thing, Ole doesn't hear very well. Besides that, he had a small air-cooled motor running, and was sharpening some of his tools.

The next thing I remember, I was being turned completely over. I was lifted clear off the ground and I landed on my stomach. By then, I was just about naked. I saw a clump of alders right ahead of me. I tried to crawl in among them. I guess I managed to move about two feet and bang! He hit me with one of his paws on the back of the skull. I didn't know at the time, but off came a piece of my scalp. About three or four inches were torn. Then he bit me across the neck, and for a few seconds I could see black discs in front of my eyes. My head sounded like a freight train rumbling through a tunnel.

I turned over on my back to see his big mouth, which was wide open. He grabbed my face with his lower jaw directly under my own jaw. His upper teeth clamped down, just under my right eye. Then he bit right through my face, cutting off part of the right side of my nose, cutting my face completely in two, including the upper lip. This crushed my lower jaw, and dislodged four of my lower teeth. A couple of them were found later with pieces of jawbone sticking to them.

By the time that was over, I didn't care any more. I was done and I knew it. But that didn't seem to bother me, either. Nothing mattered now. But for some reason, the bear called it off just then. That was the last he did. He had cut my face in half.

It seemed very quiet all of a sudden. No more growling, hitting, biting, and snorting. Slowly I began to think clearly, and slowly I looked all around. Slowly I began to wonder if I still had a chance. I lay quiet for about a minute. I listened, but all I could hear was Ole's motor over at his cabin. I managed to raise up to a sitting position. I looked and listened for another minute or two, but there was no sign of a bear.

Now what to do? What could I do? I really had no idea. There wasn't much to see except torn flesh and blood. No matter where I looked, there was blood. I could see that my right thigh was a terrible-looking sight. It looked just like so much hamburger. Anyway, I had to try my luck at moving five hundred yards.

First, I tried crawling on hands and knees. But it didn't work very well. A broken wrist bothered me, and brush punched at my badly torn thigh. I managed to get to my feet. I could move, and that was just about all. That right leg did not seem to be there. I just kind of hopped along on the left leg and dragged the right one.

I had a terrible time breathing, as the blood from my torn mouth was running down my throat. When I bent over to let the blood run out of my mouth and torn face, the blood from my torn scalp would run into my eyes and blind me. I would try to wipe it off with my arms and hands, but it was no use. Everything was bloody. I had to stop every few yards to rest and try to get some air into my lungs.

When I had made about a hundred yards, I began to get really scared. Now I was afraid that the damn bear would come after me again before I got over to Ole's cabin.

I was afraid to look back, but I kept plugging along the best I could. I had a terrible time breathing. I was about to choke on my own blood several times. But I finally got there.

Ole was still busy grinding tools, the little motor puffing away to beat the band. I tried to draw his attention, but I couldn't make much noise, because my upper lip was cut in two and I couldn't talk. I finally had to walk right up to him. When he did turn around to look at me, I was afraid, for a second, that he would fall over backward.

Of course he didn't know me. No clothes were left on me except part of my pants around my waist. Part of my scalp was torn off, half of my face was hanging like a flipper on the right side. My windpipe was exposed right under my jaw, and I'm sure there wasn't one inch on my whole body that wasn't covered with blood. No one could possibly know me. Ole told me later that he recognized only my eyes.

CHAPTER NINETEEN

KNOW YOUR ENEMY

My bear story is a true one. You can hear bear stories almost anywhere you go, but a lot of them are made up. If you ever tangle with an Alaskan Grizzly, you'll need my friend Lady Luck to see you through.

I've spent a good many years next door to Mr. Grizzly. I can tell you a lot about him, and sometimes I kind of think he was getting wise to me. So in gangster fashion, he decided, "That damn Knut. He knows too much about us. We better wipe him out. We'll make it a point to get him sometime when he is not packing that old 30.06. He has made a terrible mess of some of our relatives with that rusty musket."

So a bunch of grizzly volunteers were on the lookout for me all over Upper Copper River and the Slana River districts. One of them finally did pin me down bare-handed. But his fellow grizzlies most likely took him for a ride when they found that Knut Peterson was still alive. Not only that, in less than two years he was back in the hills

72

again. Packing that same mean-looking 30.06. He carried a .357 Magnum six-shooter besides. And killed poor innocent grizzlies without reason or warning.

Books by the dozens have been written about grizzly bears. Some of them will tell you that the grizzlies are absolutely harmless. But, in so doing, the authors only succeed in exposing their ignorance. If you prefer to believe the authors of these books, that's your business. I'd like to advise you to change your mind. If you happen to get out where the grizzlies live, at least take the book along with you. When you discover that you are in grizzly country, you can read that part of it every once in a while. You can assure yourself that you are okay, providing that guy knew what he was talking about. No, never mind the book, leave it at home, or throw it in the fireplace.

If you are going into grizzly country, bring a powerful gun and plenty of shells. If you don't want to kill bears, you may not have to use it. But I can assure you that you'll feel a whole lot better carrying the gun instead of the book. If the bear could read the book, it might be some protection to you. When he came to where it said, "The grizzly bear is harmless," he would laugh himself to death. You wouldn't have to shoot him. I intend to expose the grizzly bear for what he is. I am well aware that I'll be called a liar. But regardless of what anyone may call me, the truth remains the same.

The grizzly is protected a good part of the time by hunting ordinances. I am not sure when there is open season on him. I don't keep track of it, and I don't go hunting for him. But if he happens to show up too close to me, I declare that I may shoot him. If he attacks you or molests your property, again I would advise you not to wait until he decides to attack or molest. If he is bold enough to show up at, or near your home, get your gun for the protection of your children, providing you are lucky enough to have any. Try to get within two hundred yards of him. Don't shoot unless you can hold the gun still. The next best aim is the front shoulder, if he is at an angle to you. If you're not sure of your shot, don't pull the trigger. A wounded bear is the most dangerous of them all. If he keeps bothering you, and you're not sure of your shooting, build a smudge in a fifty-gallon drum. Keep a smoke going until you get someone else with you. With two guns, you should be able to dispose of him.

Some of the authors of the books on grizzlies claim to have made a survey of them. I never did, but I lived next door to them for over thirty years. I got to know them pretty well. I didn't study them, but I was, nevertheless, aware of their activity. I was prospecting out in the hills all those years. I put in the biggest part of my life at it.

To the authors of the books that claim that the grizzly is harmless, I would like to point out that a bullet fired from a high-powered rifle is harmless too, unless you happen to be in its path. The same goes for the grizzly. If he happens to be in a bad mood, then, just like the bullet, he doesn't care who you are. If he decides to charge, he'll come at you, roaring and frothing at the mouth. Nothing but a heavy slug will stop him. It's a good idea to let him have a few more after he is down to make sure that he is down. And to make sure that he stays down.

Very few people have seen a grizzly when he charges. A lot of those who saw it didn't live to tell about it. There is really no way to explain it so that another person can realize what it is like. I've seen it, and I can only say that it is a horrible thing to experience. It is much better that you don't realize what it is like. It is not pleasant to think about. And once you have experienced it, it is hard to forget about.

When I first moved out into the hills, I didn't pay much attention to the grizzly. That is, any more than to the other animals. I soon found out that the longer I knew him the less I liked him. I've seen him kill moose, caribou, and sheep. I've found evidence of where he killed black bears. I've watched him from a high hill through a pair of field glasses, following a cow moose, just to get newborn calves as soon as they are born. More than once, I've come home to my little tent camp, and found it all torn up and everything in it completely ruined. Then I had to walk thirty or forty miles out to the road with little or no food in my pack.

After the killing I have seen the grizzly do, I am convinced that he is also a man killer. Ever since my narrow escape, I always feel that I may have saved a life when I kill a grizzly.

We all know the reason the grizzly is protected by law. This is to get hunters from the lower states up here on big game hunts. Okay, there are lots of them here. Come on, hunters! However, in my opinion, the residents of Alaska, especially those who live along the highways, should be given the privilege of disposing of any grizzly prowling around their homes. Why hang onto a bunch of silly rules until someone gets killed or crippled? There are millions of acres of hunting ground away from the highway. For the right of a resident to protect himself and his family, change the rules. At least give a man as much right as an animal. With the present population as large as it is, it's going to be changed sometime. Why wait until some-body gets killed? Do it now!

It scares me now when I think of some of the things I used to do before I got hurt. When panning for gold on a creek, I often set my gun against a boulder and kept panning on upstream. Often, I was about a mile away from my weapon. I wouldn't do that now. You never know when you'll need a gun. And if you do need it, you need it bad! The grizzly is the king of all the animals of Alaska. He is not frightened of anything. He has no regular habits. You never know what he'll do next. He has killed quite a few people in Alaska, often for no reason at all. Of course, there have been times when a man started it and the bear finished it. The bear can't help being what he is, but don't feel sorry for him. He doesn't feel sorry for you. Don't wound him. When you do shoot him, make sure you kill him.

There is a fifty-dollar bounty on wolves because they are killers. Still, the wolf isn't classified with the grizzly. A lone wolf is a big coward. When the wolves want to make a kill, they will howl for several days. They call each other to get a pack together. Not so, Mr. Grizzly. He is fully able to handle the job himself.

Every day I see the marks of a damn mad grizzly who had no reason whatever to butcher me up. It may happen to anyone. You don't have to go hunting for him, but if you happen to be in his way when he is raving mad about something, you'll be a terrible looking mess in less than a minute. You need to have a heavy gun and be well prepared to take care of him, since he is not always alone. I've seen as many as four in one group. Some of the Indians tell me they have seen seven or eight together. That is usually in the fall, when they're digging peavine roots on the bars.

If my accident had happened a few years before, when there were no roads, you never would have heard of it. Even if it had happened a few miles from the road, I wouldn't have lived to tell about it. Throughout the years a lot of people have disappeared in the hills, not only of Alaska but in other states. I am willing to bet that the grizzly can account for a lot of them. I would like to prevent a similar accident from happening to someone. If this does warn other people, I'll feel some satisfaction in having gone through all the miseries and suffering I did.

I've been asked to tell about this accident hundreds of times. I've told it so often that I'm tired of my own voice. Often, after telling it, I've finished by saying just what I thought of the grizzly. Once, after calling him a sneaky s.o.b., a woman told me that I must not feel bitter toward the bears. She thought I should be happy to be alive. I told her that she had a lot more to be thankful for, since an experience like that never befell her. I appreciate my good health, and all the good things life has to offer.

It is a good thing that when a bad accident does hit one of us, all the rest will do everything in their power to save our life. These people keep fighting for your life, even when you give up. But somehow, I just can't get myself to feel thankful that that mad grizzly didn't finish the job of killing me. It was his intention to do so. When he left me, he was no doubt satisfied that the job was done.

A lot of people fought for my life that day, and the fight was carried on in the hospital for a long time.

So, if you are in the habit of taking chances in grizzly country without a gun, I hope, after reading of my accident, that you will feel a lot safer by carrying a gun. You may never need it, but it is much better to have one. I found that out the hard way.

CHAPTER TWENTY

BEAR IN CAMP

Now for a true bear story on the lighter side.

In 1927, I worked for the Alaska Road Commission, on a small project. The camp I worked in consisted of about twelve men, four horses, a small grader, and a couple of the old-type horse scrapers. We cut right-of-way through the spruce forest with saws and axes, and pulled the stumps with horses. It was a tent camp, and whenever it got to be too far to go to work, we moved the camp ahead.

Our cook, a cranky Old Dutchman, was having an awful time with the bears. They would sneak into camp at night and break the screen on his meat cache and pack the meat away. So he borrowed the foreman's 30.06 rifle, and he was laying for them.

One day at noon when the crew was having dinner, the cook looked out of the cook tent and spotted a big brown bear right in the camp yard. He grabbed the rifle and beat it out there. The bear was on one side of a wagon, and the cook on the other. They looked at each other through the wheels. The cook lined up on him between the wagon spokes, and shot him right through the heart. When he came back in, he hung the gun up on a nail and said, "Now they tell me that a bear is awful smart. But I found out that they are not so goddamn smart. He could see me through the wagon spokes, but he didn't think I could see him."

CHAPTER TWENTY-ONE

ADVICE

They say that anyone who is willing to take advice usually doesn't need it, and the one who needs it won't take it. But in this far north country, it is well to listen to anyone who has been here a long time, especially if you are new up here, and intend to hit for the wilderness for some reason or other. If some old timer warns you about something, he is not trying to be smart. He knows what he is talking about, and he hates to think of anybody getting in trouble if there is anything he can do to prevent it. So by all means, listen to what he tells you. It may save your life. I remember one instance when good advice was not taken.

Many years ago when gold mining and prospecting and trapping were the main businesses in the interior, there were usually some new prospectors coming up from the states every once in a while, and they all had big dreams about heavy paystreaks. And so it was that two young boys about twenty years old appeared at Copper Center Roadhouse one winter about Christmastime. They said they wanted to go to the head of the Copper River and prospect for gold. They didn't have any dogs, and they said they would pull their outfit themselves on the ice. So they bought a Yukon sled, a small tent and camp stove, groceries and other supplies. The weather was unusually mild for that time of the year, and when they were about ready to leave with a load big enough for a horse to pull, some of the old timers noticed that they both wore high-top leather shoes, and they asked the kids if they had footgear. The boys said, "No, that's all we need."

The old timers said, "Oh, no, boys, don't go up the river like that. It's over a hundred miles to where you are going. You'll get wet at times, so you need shoepacks, moccasins, lots of good wool socks and insoles. You'll run into strong, cold winds on your trip. You need good parkas, and it may get so cold that you'll have to set up your tent in the woods alongside the river and sit out a long, cold spell."

The old timers almost begged them to buy what clothing and extra footwear they knew the boys would need. They even offered them a couple of pairs of shoepacks to take along. But the boys just laughed and said, "Don't worry about us. We're okay. We'll make it."

They had no idea how wrong they were. There was nothing anyone could do. There is no law against taking off for the hills under any condition, even if it amounts to suicide. When you have done all you can to prevent it, that's all you can do. And here is what happened to the two young boys.

They got up the river about fifty or sixty miles. The temperature dropped from twenty above zero to fifty-five below. They had pulled the load off the river and into the woods, and there some Indian trapper later found them. They had attempted to build a fire. All their matches had been struck where they had tried to get a small bunch of dry spruce boughs to burn, and they had unburned matches in their frozen hands. They waited too long, and got so cold that they couldn't do anything. And it was found that they had gotten their feet wet and they most likely had frozen feet before they got off the river. They are still over there, as they were buried where they were found. The place is almost directly across the Copper River from the Chestochina Roadhouse, alongside the road on the Upper Copper River. The place is known as Dead Man's Point.

CHAPTER TWENTY-TWO

FIFTY-EIGHT BELOW—AND DROPPING

Today I see lots of boys running around with their high-powered Snowgos at ten to twenty-five miles per hour. It's a handy little rig, but look out for water, tricky river ice and overflow. If you go very far, don't forget your snowshoes and something to eat, lots of matches, and a good ax. There is always the possibility that you may have to walk back. And in case you have to camp out overnight, you never know what will happen before morning. It can snow so heavily that you can't move without snowshoes, and it can get so cold that it will keep you busy cutting wood to keep warm. Take no chance on the weather—always be prepared for the worst. I know from my own experience how fast the temperature can change.

It was the winter of 1934-1935. My brother and I were mining on the big Eldorado Creek in Chisana, a placer mining camp at the headwaters of the Chisana River. It was open cut mining in the summertime, and in the winter we hunted, trapped, and did our hauling with our dog team.

Without a dog team, we couldn't have gotten wood, lumber, groceries and other supplies up on the mining claim, which was located high above timber.

Right after Christmas that winter a prospector by the name of Jim Rogers wanted to go down to a creek called Carden Creek, about fifty miles away, and prospect for quartz. He was looking for somebody to take him and his outfit down there for him. We decided to take him down, as we intended to go down that way, anyway, and get some meat. And we had a powerful team of dogs. His outfit amounted to about four hundred pounds, and the first day we made twenty-five miles down the Chisana River to a place called King City where there was a cabin. The next day we hunted and killed a moose close to the cabin, and we hauled in the meat. The next day we took off across country on a twenty-five mile trip to Cardin Creek. Jim and I broke trail with snowshoes and my brother, Ulrick, followed with the team. The temperature was four below zero that morning when we left King City. It was a nice clear day, and we thought we could make Carden Creek that night, where there was an old cabin that Jim intended to use for his living quarters while prospecting.

We could all feel it was getting colder and colder by the hour that forenoon. It was hard pulling for the dogs in the loose snow, and Jim and I got a long way ahead of them. We lost sight of them, but it got so cold that we could see a cloud of steam rising up in the air, so we knew exactly where they were. About noon we built a small fire and waited for my brother and the team.

We always had a thermometer taped right to the sled, and when my brother got there, we found that it was fifty-eight below zero. We had a cup of hot tea and a cold hamburger. We couldn't stop very long, and we knew then that we would never make it to Carden Creek. We were less than halfway, and it gets dark about two-thirty that time of the year. So we agreed to keep going until about two o'clock and be on the lookout for a spot of dry wood.

Luck was really with us there. About two o'clock we came to a place where there had been a forest fire, and there was all kinds of dry wood around. Not only that, but we found out that it was all good sound and solid wood. Almost every tree was rotten at the root, and we could just tip them over by pushing against them. That was the handiest place for firewood I've ever run across.

We made camp, and by then it was sixty-four below zero. In a few minutes we had a roaring fire going. We made spruce bough beds for each of the dogs and fed them a nice chunk of moose meat. It was also a lucky break that the three of us had lots of experience and nobody got excited.

Nobody goes out on the trail at sixty-four below. But when you get caught out there, you are in it, and you'll have to do the best you can to put up with it. We had lots of good clothing, and we were all young, strong, and healthy. And so was our team of dogs. We had Jim's outfit on the sled plus a big chunk of fresh moose meat.

We must have tipped over three or four cords of wood. We kept busy firing, cooking, and packing in wood, after cutting it to whatever size we could handle. We cut a big stack of spruce boughs, and about midnight we spread out sleeping robes on top of them, buttoned them together, crawled into them with most of our clothes on and slept six hours. There were still lots of hot coals when we got up. For breakfast we had moose steak, coffee, and then we boiled some hard frozen eggs. It was still sixty-four below zero. We talked about camping there another day, but at nine a.m., we hooked up the team and took off. We made the cabin on Carden Creek at one p.m. It was still sixty-four below; it seemed like it was anchored on sixty-four.

The next day we rested at the cabin, firing in the stove and talking about million dollar gold mines. That afternoon the weather broke, and the next morning it was only five below zero. We had a good trail and nice weather going back with the empty sled. We took turns on the handle bars, one of us riding in the sled.

I've told that true experience a few times at parties when the conversation happened to be along that line. And so have Jim Rogers and my brother. We all had the same results. Somebody would wink at somebody else, meaning, of course, "Try to beat that for b.s."

So we don't tell it anymore. At least, not to anyone who had never been out on a trip across country, where there was nobody in the world to depend on but themselves. I am telling it here because it's a cold fact, and one that you should know and always remember in case you happen to be the type who may some day take off for the wilderness of Alaska on a mild winter day. If not, remember it anyway. You may have a chance some day to warn somebody else. When you leave the highway, whichever way you travel—afoot, horseback dog team, Snowgo or any other way—you'll soon discover that Alaska is as it always was—a challenge! It favors no one, but it appeals to a lot of us. It has always been fascinating to me, and it will be as long as I live.

But, one thing I learned early here; it pays to listen to some well-meant advice at times. While it is true that the temperature doesn't very often change that fast, it is also true that it can happen. You should always be prepared for the worst, regardless of how nice the weather may be.

CHAPTER TWENTY-THREE

TWELVE MISSING,

AND THEY DISAPPEARED

I personally know of at least twelve men who disappeared in the wilderness of Alaska. None of them was ever found, except part of Tony McGettigen, whose left foot was found with the shoepack still on it. The rest of his body was never discovered. Tony was about seventy-five years old, an average good-sized man, but not very strong at that age.

Another one of the twelve was Ole Olsen, who was past eighty when he disappeared. The other ten were healthy and strong, and most of them about middle-age. I knew quite a few of them, but I didn't know them all. We know that at least one of them was drowned, but we have no idea what happened to most of them.

I often think of these men for the simple reason that if my accident had happened almost any place but where it did, I would be part of that list myself. Every year somebody disappears in Alaska without leaving a trace, but with the plane service available now, a search can be made so much quicker, and many lives can be rescued.

Here are the stories, with the few facts available, of the twelve men.

William Heimer prospected at the headwater of the Copper River in the early 1920's. He came down the river on the ice one spring, pulling a small hand sled, and bought some groceries and clothes from Lawrence DeWitt, who had a trading post at the mouth of the Slana River.

Some of the goods he bought from DeWitt were found in his camp months later when a search was made for him, so they knew he had made it back to his camp. But Bill Heimer was never found.

Neal Phillips and Joe Veil prospected and trapped on the LaDue River in the 1920's. One spring day they decided to build a cabin at a place where they had lived in a tent. After a big moose steak dinner that they had one day at noon, Neal told Joe that he was going out to look around for trees that were big enough for cabin logs. He took a small ax with him to mark them with.

He didn't show up at supper time, and Joe went looking for him. He called for Neal at the top of his voice, and late that evening fired his gun, but got no results.

The next morning, Joe panicked. He found sixteen trees that Neal had marked with his little ax, but he never found the hand ax, and there was no sign of Neal or any indication of what might have happened to him.

After searching fruitlessly most of the summer with the help of some natives, Joe packed up and left Alaska. He told the natives, "I am leaving this country before it gets me too."

Also in the twenties, Alvin Thorson prospected at the headwaters of the Chestochina River. One day in July, he came to Slate Creek and bought some groceries and tobacco from the Slate Creek Mining Company. That was the last time anyone ever saw him. Somebody found his little tent on a small creek in the fall, but there was no sign that he had been there for weeks. No trace of him was ever found.

Dale Mark prospected on the Upper Tok River in the twenties. Like Alvin Thorson, he came to Middle Fork Mining Company, which was about fifty miles from where he prospected. He bought groceries, ammunition, and tobacco. He was never heard of again. His camp was found, but it appeared that he had never gotten back to it after he left the Middle Fork Mining Company.

Mike Cutter had a big cabin alongside the Gakona River about twenty miles from the road. I knew Mike pretty well. Once he tried to talk me into going into partnership with him. He raised foxes, planted a big garden every summer, and had a nice little buckskin pony that he used to ride when he came out to the Gakona Trading Post for his mail and the few things he needed. He finally sold his foxes and gave up the idea of raising them. But he kept gardening in the summer and trapping in the winter.

It was about 1935 when some of his friends decided that it had been too long since Mike had been out to the trading post. They went to investigate, but Mike was gone. The party who went in search of him spent a few days at his cabin, and they said it appeared that he had been gone for a long time. He was never heard of again. Just what happened to his pretty little pony, I never did find out.

Herman Stiller prospected and trapped on the Upper Gulkana River in the 1920's. One spring while the ice was still good, he came down to Gulkana Trading Post, sold his fur, bought some groceries and other supplies. Then he

89

hired an Indian with a dog team to haul his stuff to his summer camp, where he intended to prospect all summer.

In July, two new prospectors came across his camp. It had been completely demolished by bears, and there was no sign that anyone had been there for a long time. The news came out to the road. A search party volunteered to go in there. But Herman was never found.

Lawrence DeWitt owned and operated a roadhouse and trading post at the mouth of the Slana River, along the Nabesna Road, where my brother and I would visit when we were mining in Chisana. He was married to a native woman and they had several children. One morning in the spring or early summer of 1935 or 1936, he left his place of business and walked up the river a ways. They found his tracks on the sandbars of the river, apparently leading into the stream. They never did find him.

Tony McGettigen, an old friend of mine, was mining on Bonanza Creek in Chisana when my brother and I came there to mine in 1933. We mined there five years, and Tony was still there when we left. He had a cabin in what was called the town of Chisana, which was really more of a winter quarters for the miners. But he also owned a claim on Upper Bonanza Creek.

It was during World War II when Tony was on his way up to his claim, about a ten or twelve mile walk. Someone else had hauled his supplies up for him. And all he had to do was walk up there by following the pack trail which was pretty good walking, although fairly steep. Tony intended to stay overnight with a friend of his about half-way. This would give him two days to get up to his claim, but he was never to see that claim again.

He failed to show up at his friend's camp, and they

went to look for him the next day. They found his little packsack under a spruce tree on the upper side of the trail. Right below the trail, they found his shoepack with his foot and part of his leg in it. Just what happened, nobody will ever know. The ground was too dry to detect any animal tracks. We know where he died, and that is all.

Bob Long was another friend of mine who prospected in Chisana for a while, and he also worked for some of the miners. In the spring of 1935, he left the little mining community while the ice was still good on the river, with two sled dogs and a small sled. He headed for Scottie Creek about sixty or seventy miles downstream on the Chisana river, where he intended to prospect for quartz all summer. Someone else left with a dog team on the same route a few days later. He could see Bob's track in the snow most of the way until he got down about forty miles. There he lost them. He made a search, but that seemed to be the end of the trail for Bob.

There was an Indian village at the mouth of Scottie Creek, and they hadn't seen him, either. So everybody figured that something had happened to him, or he had changed his mind and struck off across country for some other place, but that didn't seem likely, because he had only enough supplies with him to last for the trip to Scottie Creek.

In June, one of his dogs came back to Chisana, almost starved to death. The other one was found dead on the river bar about twenty miles down the river, studded with porcupine quills. Bob Long was never found. He was a big, strong, healthy man about thirty-five years old. Of course, none of us know what happened to him. But we all know that a dog will never leave his master out in the wilderness,

91

even for a long time after the master is done.

In 1937, Dan Stacy prospected at the headwaters of the Nabesna River. He waded across the river to do some work. By the time he got ready to cross back again, the river had risen several feet. He was never seen again, but they did find his tracks on the sandbar where he had entered the river to cross it, so we know he drowned, although his body was never found.

Ole Olsen, old-time prospector, miner and trapper, lived in his cabin along the Tanana River near Tanacross. He was an old man when he disappeared a few years after the end of World War II. He had evidently been missing for a long time before anybody thought much about it. No trace of him was ever found.

I can't recall Cunningham's first name, but in the 1950's he left the Taylor Highway in the Forty-Mile country and struck off across country with a pack on his back. Nobody seemed to know just what he intended to do or where he was headed. No one has seen him since.

CHAPTER TWENTY-FOUR

TWO "TRAPPERS"

For obvious reasons, I'll have to use fictitious names in this story, which involves both people and also places of residence. The Richardsen Highway, Copper Center, Culkana, and Mrs. Griffet are the only names that are real. The story is a true one.

George Barter and Mike Stein were both crackerjack trappers, or at least so they said. George had a cabin along the Richardsen Highway at a place called Stone Creek, which he called his headquarters. Forty miles north of there, Mike had his headquarters, also right alongside the highway. They were both hooked onto the telephone line, so they could talk to each other or anybody else along the road. This was the old Signal Corps telephone built by the Army along the old narrow gravel and dirt road. Each party had an assigned ring, such as one long and two shorts, and so on.

George and Mike knew each other real well. They were both old-timers in Alaska. In 1925, George was sixty-nine and Mike was sixty-four years old. George was known as "Loud-mouth George," and Mike's handle was "Windbag Mike." When they were together, they were the best of friends, but as soon as they were apart, they would talk to other people about each other and call each other names. George would say about Mike: "Oh, that big windbag. Don't pay any attention to him." And Mike talked the same way about George. The funny part about George and Mike was that they called themselves trappers. But they were actually professional moonshiners and too old to do any trapping, anyway.

Everybody along the road knew that the handle, "trapper", was just a blind. There was a good demand for moonshiners in those dry years, and most of the moonshiners had their market pretty well established before they set up business.

Throughout the long, cold winter months, people along the road usually called each other on the phone every day, and while two parties were talking, all the rest would listen in. Of course, they all said they never did listen in, and they also knew that they were all lying. At any rate, at the end of each day everybody knew all the news along the line. They knew who had been at the trading post and brought in a nice, big bundle of furs; that Chief Longneck's squaw had given birth to a baby boy; that a white trapper had brought a lot of moonshine into some Indian village and got them all drunk. And whoever had a telephone would know exactly what they were having for supper at a trading post a hundred miles away.

Mail was brought out from Chitina, which was head quarters for the Alaska Road Commission, twice a month, and the day after mail day was a busy day on the phone, with everyone telling everyone else the news they had received in the mail. George and Mike usually called each other once a week, and the conversation would go something like this:

"Hello, Mike, how goes it?"

"Oh, fine. I just got home yesterday. I only caught two cross-foxes."

And George would say, "Oh, well, that's not too bad. I didn't get anything this week."

Everybody was listening, and they all knew it was just so much talk to keep the blinds down.

The next day someone would call Mike. "Hi, there. How goes it over your way?"

"Oh, not too bad. How are you all at your place?"

"Okay. I heard George caught a couple of silver foxes."

"Oh, he is a damn liar. I just talked to him yesterday, and he told me he didn't get anything this week."

The party would say, "He told Indian Charlie that he caught them."

"I don't care who he told it to. You can't believe a damn word of what he tells you."

And of course George was listening in. But then George always said that he never listened in on anybody's conversation. And not only that, he insisted that he had no use for anyone who would listen in on anybody else's private dialogue. Mike had made a similar statement, and George kind of thought that Mike was the only one who didn't listen in. So they both kind of depended on each other not to listen in on the phone.

The long, cold winter months went slowly by. It was the spring of 1925, and after being penned in their cabins all winter, everybody was afflicted with "cabin fever." The road had been closed all winter except for the Snowmobile that had been bringing out the mail.

Everybody was like a tight-strung wire ready to snap any minute. George and Mike had been telling everybody along the road what a dirty skunk the other one was, both of them depending on the other not to listen in. And they were both like steam boilers about to blow up.

Then one day in May, George called Mrs. Griffet at Gulkana Roadhouse and Trading Post. She had been in business for many years, and we always called her Ma Griffet.

"Hello, George," she said. "How are you?"

"Oh, just fine, Ma."

"Isn't it nice, George, to see that old sun back with us again after all those short, cold days?"

"Indeed it is, Ma."

"Oh, say, George, how is Mike getting along?"

George said, "Oh, there was an Indian came by here a few days ago. And the way I understand it, Mike is like he always was—drunk most of the time."

Finally, Mike couldn't stand it any longer, and he spoke up loud and clear, "That's a goddamn lie, you dirty bastard!"

George said, "Hold it, Mike. Hold it. We are using the line, and watch your language, Mike there is a lady on the line."

Mike bellowed, "You lowdown s.o.b."

Now Mrs. Griffet spoke up. "Don't be like that, boys. What's the matter with you?

George got a word in again. "Don't pay any attention to him, Ma. I told you he is drunk."

Mike was roaring like a lion. "Who is drunk?"

George said, "You are. Who else? And I have a witness here on this very line who heard you call me a s.o.b.

You don't call me that, Mike, and get away with it. Better get all your papers in order, Mike. If you don't have a will made out, better do so. Next time I see you, I'll have a gun and I'll shoot you on sight whether you carry a gun or not."

Ma Griffet spoke up again. "You act like a couple of crazy schoolboys. I can't stand it any longer. I am hanging up."

The telephone clicked, but George and Mike were a long way from hanging up. Mike cut loose again. "So you are challenging me to a fight, George. Good deal. You can sure make yourself sound awful brave while there is a lady listening in. I don't think you know me, George. I don't think you know that I've had to shoot my way through life, which is the cause of several graves throughout Arizona. Don't worry, George. I'll have my old .44, and whatever you are packing means exactly nothing to me. Whatever it is, you'll never pack it again. You asked for it, George. And you are going to get it!"

George said, "Okay, Mike. We understand each other now. Let us not wait forever for this to happen. If I get a chance to hitch a ride up to your palce, I'll call you before I leave here. And you do the same if you can hitch a ride down here. That gives us a fair chance and the sooner we get this over with, the better."

"Okay," said Mike. "All terms agreed to."

Now the silent gossip was in high gear all along the line. Nobody wanted to talk about it on the phone, as they didn't want George and Mike to listen. Everybody had heard the duel challenge on the phone, and they were all looking for excitement. It had been a long, dull winter. Boy, oh, boy! Look out now! Big gun fight coming up! Indian runners carried messages and letters from one place to the next. The snow was off the road, but it was wet and

97

muddy. A few of the residents along the road had light cars.

George and Mike had no idea about the excitement they had caused. They didn't think anybody knew about it except Mrs. Griffet. And she had hung up, so she hadn't heard the result of the hot argument.

It was about the middle of May when a light Ford car pulled up in front of trapper Mike Stein's cabin one forenoon. The first car of the season. A young man who had been a chore boy for Mrs. Griffet at Gulkana during the winter months was driving it.

Mike came out and shook hands with the young man. "Hello, there, Fred. It sure is nice to see some of the neighbors again. Where are you going, Fred, and how far do you think you can go?"

Fred said, "Ma Griffet wants me to go to Tonsina, if I can make it. Mrs. Yeager has a bundle of fur that she wants Mrs. Griffet to ship together with hers. But I may not be able to get through the drifts on the hill. She told me to stop here on the way back and pick up a five-gallon keg of moonshine. Here is a note she sent to you."

"Come on in, Fred, and have a drink, or would you rather have a cup of coffee?"

"Coffee will do."

Mike poured himself a drink and a cup of coffee for Fred. And then he said to Fred, "I would like to ride with you as far as George Barter's place."

Fred said, "Okay, Mike. I'll be glad to have you along."

Mike poured himself another drink and then he said: "Fred, I have a dirty job to do today. I am going to kill a man." And he told Fred all about it.

Fred acted kind of scared, but Mike said. "Don't you worry, Fred. You don't even have to see it. Just let me off

98

when we get close to George's, and you keep right on going."

Mike went to the phone to call George. He rang and rang, but there was no answer. And that went on for half an hour. Every few minutes he rang and rang, but nothing happened. So he said. "Oh, to hell with it. I'll go anyway. I'm in a fighting mood now, and something has to give." He strapped on his old .44, and slipped a pint of moonshine into his hip pocket, and they left.

It was slow going, as the road was soft and there were several water and mud puddles where they had to ease through in low gear. Old Mike tilted the bottle several times as they rolled along, and he began to kind of worry about old George.

"I just can't understand it," he said, "why he didn't answer the phone. I kind of wonder if there is anything wrong. I remember he had some sort of a spell about two years ago, and I am beginning to think now that it might have been his heart. Wouldn't that be awful if he is laying there in his cabin half-paralyzed and me coming down here to shoot him? Oh, why didn't I call everybody along the line to ask them if they had talked to George lately."

He asked Fred if he knew of anyone who had talked to George on the phone the last couple of days, but Fred said, "No."

Mike took another drink as they climbed a ridge where they could see George's cabin below. They stopped the car and took a good look. There was no sign of life and no smoke coming out of the stovepipe.

Mike was half-drunk, and he said, "It looks mighty empty down there, Fred. But let us go on down. You let me off just before we get to the cabin, and you drive on by. If you don't come back today, don't worry about me."

They drove down close to the place. Mike got off and Fred drove on. What he really did was drive just far enough to get the car out of sight. Then he walked back and in through the woods right back of George's cabin, and climbed a tall spruce tree to watch the show.

It was about noon when Mike stood in front of the cabin and listened. But there was no sound. He thought to himself: Something must have happened to poor George. Goddamn me! Why the hell did I come here? He knocked on the door. No answer. He opened it and looked inside. No sign of life. Then he slowly walked around the building to the back side facing south and the sun. And there, in a homemade easy chair, sat George Barter, his head sort of slumping down, his pipe laying on the ground between his feet! Mike lost control of himself.

"Mike Stein," he said out loud, "Goddamn you, Mike! I hate you! Yes, I do! I hate myself! Why was I ever born?" And then, "Oh, look, look, why George is moving!"

Slowly, George raised his sleepy head, rubbed his eyes and face. He looked at Mike and blinked, a surprised look on his face.

"Why, Mike, you old rascal, you. Am I seeing things, or is it real? Well, I'll be a son of a gun. It really is old Mike in person."

They almost had tears in their eyes as they shook hands and said, "Well, well, well."

"By God, but it's good to see you, old boy," said Mike.

"And the same to you," said George.

"You sure had me scared for a while, George. Sitting there with your head slumping down as if it was going to fall off. For a while I thought you had left this world for

100

good. Now tell me, George, how did you come to sit out here in the hot sun and sleep so sound?"

"You know how it is, Mike. That spring sun feels so good, and I ran a batch of moonshine through last night. I didn't get through till nine o'clock this morning. I was tired when I sat down in the sun here to rest. Guess I must have gone to sleep. Come on in, old boy. We'll have a drink for old time's sake. Tell me, how is everything at your place, Mike, and how did you get here?"

Fred crawled down off the spruce tree, got into the car, drove to the nearest telephone, and the news was on the wire.

After a few drinks, George said, "Now, Mike, if there is anything you're short of, I am well stocked with everything. And anything I have is yours."

"Oh, no, George. I've got plenty of everything at my place. I just had to come and see what might be wrong after ringing for hours without getting an answer."

And then Fred showed up with the car. He said he couldn't get through the snowdrifts on the hill.

George said, "Why don't you two guys stay here tonight? I've got lots of room, lots of food, and lots of booze. And you are welcome as the flowers in May."

"Oh no, thanks a million just the same, but I just have to get back home. There are so many things to do now before the traffic starts and a lot of nosy guys come around."

"Here, Mike, take this pint of booze and put it in your pocket for the road."

"Thanks, George. You must come and see me sometime. You owe me a visit now."

"I sure will as soon as the road dries up and the traffic starts. I'll hitch a ride over some day."

101

Mike said, "That's a promise now?"

George said, "That's a promise, Mike."

They shook hands and parted, and not a word had been said about any shooting.

When Mike got home he said to himself, after Fred had left: "Oh, Christ, I've been wearing that damn old .44 all day without even noticing it myself."

Then he called Ma Griffet and told her that Fred was on the way back and that he had a package for her.

"Oh, say, Ma," he said, "I went with Fred as far as George's place."

"Oh", she said, "and how is our friend George?"

"Oh, he is the same old loud-mouthed liar that he always was."

Ma said, "Oh, now, Mike, that's an awful thing to say."

CHAPTER TWENTY-FIVE

TAZILINA ROADHOUSE,
DOC BLAYLOCK, OWNER AND OPERATOR

Doc Blaylock owned one of the roadhouses along the old Richardsen Highway. He was a big man, weighing over three hundred pounds. He was the only person who operated a roadhouse all alone, along that road, but in the wintertime he usually had some trapper staying with him, helping him with his wood, giving him a hand when he ran through a batch of whiskey, and helping him drink some of it. He had been a veterinarian at one time, and so they always called him Doc.

Doc Blaylock's whiskey was known all along the road. It was in a class by itself. If anybody poured you a drink of Doc's product and you said, "By golly, that's good moonshine," they would get sort of peeved and say, "Moonshine, hell! This is whiskey. Doc Blaylock's whiskey."

Doc himself, as good-natured as he was, would get sore if you called it moonshine. "You are drinking whiskey here, son," he would say, "and don't you forget it. I challenge any distiller in the world to beat my brand."

The first time I met Doc was in 1926. I took a liking to him right away. There was something about him, comfortableness, generosity, or whatever it was, that made everybody take an instant liking to Doc Blaylock. His so-called roadhouse was about the most untidy, filthy place I've ever seen. He had a homemade rocking chair, where he spent most of his time, watching a fifty-gallon barrel of mash fermenting right back of the cookstove in the kitchen. We used to joke about it, saying that regardless of how dark and stormy it was, you could never miss Doc's place because you could smell your way to it.

There was one thing Doc was very particular about. That was his still. It was the only thing in the house that was really clean. He insisted on taking care of that himself, and he sure did make good whiskey. He sold quite a bit, he gave a lot of it away, and he drank a lot of it himself.

It was always the same when you came into his place of business.

"Hello, Doc."

"Why, hello, there, son. Look at your rosy cheeks. They talk about a picture of health—you must be it."

"How have you been, and how are you?"

"Welcome to my horrible-looking dump. Grab a chair, a box, or a block of wood, and sit down while you are thinking up all the news. I'll get us a drink."

After a few drinks and exchanging ideas, the visitor would probably say:

"How about some supper, Doc, and can you put me up for the night?"

"Why, God bless your heart, son. You can stay as long as you wish. I've got lots of grub, and you'll find a bunk upstairs. Whenever you get hungry, help yourself to anything you find in the kitchen."

When you got hungry enough, you fixed up some sort of a meal. And when you were about ready to eat, Doc would come out in the kitchen and say, "That smells mighty good, son. I believe, by golly, I'll just have a plate with you myself. But we better have a couple of shots first."

That was how he operated his roadhouse. The customer did the work, and when he got ready to leave and asked about his bill, Doc would say: "Well, whatever it's worth to you, son. If you're short, it's all right. Anyhow, I sure wish you could stay longer. It will be mighty lonesome now. Hope you can be here again in a few days. I'll need help to run off a batch of whiskey."

And so it went at Doc's place from week to week, month to month, and year to year. I don't think he made any money, and he didn't lose any. But he enjoyed life. I've never known anyone to be so satisfied and contented. He always promised himself that he would start reducing about next week.

"Nothing to it," he would say. "I am a bit overweight, son. But I know just how to get rid of that. A ten-mile hike every day for a month, and I'll be back to my normal weight of one hundred ninety pounds." But he never took that ten-mile hike.

Doc always seemed to take it for granted that he could trust everybody. He mentioned it at times. "Nobody has ever done me any harm and no one ever will." One day a stranger showed up. Doc had no idea that the young man was a prohibition officer, and so when he entered his front door, Doc said to him, "Why, hello there, stranger. God bless your heart. I do believe that you saved my life. I was so lonesome I don't think I could have stood it another

105

hour. Grab yourself something to sit on. I take it that you can stand a drink after fighting that wheel on this muddy road. Will you have a glass of water with it? Well, here's to you, son."

In spite of all the filth and smell, the prohibition officer took a great liking to Doc right away, and the longer he talked to him, the better he liked him. He could no more have pinched Doc than he could have pinched his own father.

After an hour or so, he said to Doc, "Well, I must be on my way."

Doc almost had tears in his eyes. "I don't know what it is," he said, "but today I just have that lonesome feeling." He shook hands with the young man and said, "If you ever come this way again, son, you be sure to stop in."

"Okay Dad, I'll do that. Good-by now and be careful, Dad."

Shortly after the stranger had left the telephone rang. "Hello, Doc."

"Why, hello, Frank. How are you this fine day?"

"Okay, Doc. But, say, I've some important news for you. There is a prohibition officer on the road and he may call at your place. So you better hide everything in a hurry."

Doc asked Frank: "Is he a young, blond fellow driving a Ford coupe?"

Frank said, "Yes. That's the man."

Doc said: "Oh, well, Frank. He has already been here. He was such a nice young man, and I was sort of lonesome. We had a couple of drinks together, and he had coffee and a cheese sandwich. But I really don't think he suspected me of making the stuff."

Frank said, "Look out, Doc. I was into your place a

couple of days ago, and I could smell that mash of yours before I opened the door. You can never tell what will happen next, Doc. He may come back and have some other prohibition officer with him. If he was in your place, he knows you are making it. Better haul everything away some place and hide it. I'll come over and give you a hand."

But Doc said, "Oh hell, Frank. That nice young man will never do me any harm. I could see it in his eyes."

And I guess he could. At any rate, nothing ever did happen. The silent gossip came from Fairbanks that the young officer had told a good friend up there that he would rather resign from his job than arrest old Blaylock, although he admitted that he had seen him only that one time.

Doc went right on making whiskey, rocking in his old chair, smoking his old pipe, making more and more friends, and gaining more and more weight as the years went by.

When he finally got so heavy that he had to go to the hospital, somebody asked him when they hauled him away, "When will you be back, Doc?"

"Well, son," he said, "as soon as I lose some weight. And I have a strong hunch that I'll lose so much that there won't be enough left to be worth while bringing back here." And he was right; he never did come back to his roadhouse.

CHAPTER TWENTY-SIX

NECK-STRAP CASPER

Neck-Strap Casper had no use for dogs. He thought they were noisy, dirty and undependable. He had a neck strap (actually, a shoulder strap) tied to his sled and attached around his own neck and pulled his loads without dogs. He didn't like the animals, but whenever he could, he did use the trails made by teams pulling loads of freight across country on the snow.

On one occasion, six prospectors formed a company. They agreed to go to a creek, fifty miles distant, which was known to carry some gold, although nobody had tried mining it yet. They would leave in time to get their outfit hauled in on the snow, and to whipsaw some lumber for sluice boxes before break up. They would set up camp alongside of the creek, and as soon as the water started flowing, they would wash off the overburden to bedrock and find whether or not the ground would produce enough gold to make it pay. If the ground proved to be worthwhile, each would stake his individual claims. Each man had his own dog team and summer outfit.

Neck-Strap Casper was one of the party, but of course he didn't have any dogs. He stayed about a day behind, and that way he had a well-beaten trail, and he got out of breaking trail altogether.

The other five men didn't care. They all knew him, and they all got a kick out of it. They were together one night, and they knew Neck-Strap was alone back on the trail, maybe talking to himself. They also knew that if they didn't break the trail, he wouldn't be able to make it at all.

When they got to the creek and set up their tents, they shoveled the snow off on a spot for Neck-Strap to set up his tent. But when he got there he said, "Oh, to hell with it! I am not going to set my tent up here and listen to them goddamn dogs barking and howling. Oh no, I am going upstream about a mile and have my camp in a quiet and peaceful place." And so he did.

It turned out to be a late spring. They had the lumber cut for sluice boxes, and they didn't have much to do except wait for water. One sunny afternoon when Neck-Strap was lying on his narrow bunk reading, he noticed something walking right close to the side of his little tent. He thought it was one of the malemute dogs that had gotten loose, and he said, "Oh, you goddamn dirty son-of-a bitch. Get away from here!"

By then it was right up against him, but on the other side of the canvas. So he hauled off with his right fist and hit it with all his might. He had no idea that he was hitting a fair-sized black bear!

Evidently, the bear didn't appreciate that kind of greeting, so he stood up on his hind legs and let go a wallop with his right paw, down on the roof of the tent, ripping it open, and with the same swipe he tore a big piece off of Neck-Strap's new overalls.

Neck-Strap got out of that tent faster than any move he had ever made and beat it down stream at a dead gallop, without any shoes on, screaming for help at the top of his voice. The bear was so surprised that he took off at a fast clip in the opposite direction. When Neck-Strap got close to the camp of his five partners, the dogs started barking, and for once he was glad to hear dogs barking. He quit running and just walked the rest of the way in.

"That's the boys," he said, "Keep right on barking. That will keep that goddamn bear out of camp."

From that day on, for the rest of his life, he had a different attitude toward dogs.

His partners helped him move his tent and outfit back down to the main camp. After he got his tent sewed up, he bought three dogs from the other guys and tied them right close to his door. He put in a lot of his spare time petting his dogs and all the other dogs in camp. Whenever the dogs started to bark, he would be the first one out of his tent with his 30-30 rifle, ready to heed their warning.

Neck-Strap had from three to five dogs for the rest of his life, and they said he would never sleep out in the open without three dogs staked in a triangle around him. He got to be so friendly with dogs that when any of the malemute dogs in his neighborhood saw him, they would wag their tails and bark—their way of telling him to come on over and talk to them.

Soon, his partners changed his name. Instead of Neck-Strap, they named him Malemute Casper.

CHAPTER TWENTY-SEVEN

ELDORADO RED

"Gold! Gold! Gold! New discovery! Rich placer gold deposits have been found near the headwater of the Chisana River!"

So went the news from mouth to mouth throughout Alaska in the year of 1913. And in a surprisingly short time it had reached Fairbanks, Dawson, and all along the coast to Seattle. Everybody thought it was a second Klondike, and within a few weeks, thousands of stampeders were scattered and camped, roughly in a twenty-five mile square, in the vicinity of the new discovery. A log cabin town consisting of about 500 cabins sprang up about seven miles below Bonanza Creek. The streams were staked and prospected for miles around.

But it was a small plot of paying ground, and in a short time thousands of men left as suddenly as they had come, and fewer than 300 men remained to mine the few streams which were fairly rich. And as in most other mining camps, there were a few greedy characters who staked more ground than they could begin to mine, and held the claims just to keep others from staking it.

North of Bonanza Creek and across what was called Gold Hill was a creek called Big Eldorado. The largest part of it had been staked by two men, McKinney and McGettigen. They held it several years and never even went near it and no assessment work was ever done on it. A small cut had been mined on #3 below Upper Discovery, but it evidently hadn't produced enough to encourage the men to do any more work. Several parties prospected on the creek, but when they saw the location notices they walked away.

One day a big, redheaded man came along and did some panning in a small cut that somebody had tried to mine. He soon discovered that there was plenty of money in the bedrock, but it would be necessary to take up three or four feet of bedrock. This was all cracked and had to be taken up in big, flat slabs. Then clay and sediment had to be scraped and washed in order to get to the gold.

But Red Stevens didn't walk away when he looked at the location notices. He noted the date on them and then he looked for evidence of assessment work. Nothing had been done except the small cut where he had panned. That would barely be assessment work for one year on that claim and the ground had been staked for six years.

So he went down to the town of Chisana to look at the records. He found that the claims had been recorded, but no assessment work had ever been recorded. So he went back to the Big Eldorado and staked #3 and #4 below Upper Discovery. Number 3 was a wide claim. That is, the creek bed was wide and there were very few big boulders with only about three feet of gravel on top of the bedrock. And the bedrock was rich! Number 4 below, was a sort of canyon, and so was #2 at the upper end of #3. Heavy boulders were numerous on both 2 and 3.

Nobody paid much attention to Red Stevens until the next spring when it was noted that he had a big tent camp set up on #3. He had hired six men, all good workers, and he was ground sluicing to beat the band.

Soon the big cry went up. "Oh, the dirty bastard! He jumped our ground! He is a damn claim jumper! We'll show him!"

McGettigen and McKinny went to the commissioner. The marshal was called and a warrant sworn out for the arrest of Red Stevens.

Red was a miner and knew what he was doing. He washed off the gravel to bedrock, made a big, heavy dump box, and with a long, lead hose, had a steady stream of water flowing through it. With wheelbarrows the men wheeled the slabs of bedrock into the heavy dump box, scrubbed them clean and threw them out to the side.

Red Stevens was making money and lots of it. Just how much many people would have liked to know. He paid his men big wages, and they all liked to work with him. Red didn't do anything himself, to speak of. He had a hunch there would be trouble, but he didn't let it bother him. His men picked up the gossip here and there, and he knew something was about to happen.

Sure enough, one day he saw two men coming down the hillside toward his camp. He went into his tent, and when he came back out, he had a 30-30 rifle in the crook of his arm. Then he told his men, "Well, here it comes. Now you guys act like you are scared of me. They all think I am half-crazy now, and when they leave here, they'll be convinced."

113

Just as the marshal and his deputy entered the camp, Red shouted to a couple of the men and pointed the gun at a big boulder. "Get a bar and get that rock out of the way!" He shouted orders to some of the other guys, pointing the gun here and there in all directions, and the men jumped around like a bunch of scared wolves.

Finally, the marshal walked over to Red and said, "Hello."

Red said, "I am not hiring any more men. Better go over to Bonanza Creek. There is lots of mining going on over there."

"I am not looking for a job. I am the marshal and I have a warrant for your arrest. You jumped this ground."

Red turned toward the marshal, holding the 30-30 in the crook of his arm so that it was pointed right at the marshal's stomach. "Yes," he said, "I did, if that's what you want to call it, and I'll jump you in less than thirty seconds if you don't get off it!"

Red was not only a miner, but he was also a good actor, and he put on a wild look that would put a scare into anybody. The six men all wore a scared look.

The marshal and his deputy didn't wait thirty seconds. They started right back up the hillside the way they had come, walking twice as fast and never looking back. Red let out a bellow at the men once in a while, "Turn the water over there! Dig a big drain! What's the matter with you guys!"

But as soon as the marshal was out of hearing distance, Red brought out a jug and said, "We'll just call it a day, boys. I'll say one thing for you guys. You sure know how to put on a scared look, but I'll bet that marshal will have a scared look on his face from now on!"

114

Red and his crew had a little party that afternoon. Nobody ever bothered him again. McKinny and McGettigen decided that Red was not the kind of man to let a marshal and deputy, or a location notice, bluff him.

He worked the claim out in five years. Nobody ever found out how much gold he took out. All the information anybody could ever get out of him was, "Well, I am not losing any money on it."

All the Chisana miners had lots of respect for Red as long as he was in there. Even McKinny and McGettigen called him "Mr. Stevens" when they happened to meet him.

The funny part of it was that after Red pulled out, a lot of mining was done on all the other claims. But none of them produced enough to make it pay. Part of #3 was worked a second time and still paid fairly well.

No one ever found out how big a wage he paid his crew. When anybody asked them, they all gave the same answer: "Oh, we get good wages." It was later learned that they all bought nice homes near Seattle, Washington.

They called him Eldorado Red, and they said he was half crazy, but he bought a farm in Washington for a hundred thousand dollars and paid cash for it!

McKinny and McGettigen spent the rest of their lives wondering how much money they could have made on Big Eldorado.

CHAPTER TWENTY-EIGHT

BLIND MAGGIE

Eskimos and some tribes of Indians believed in letting old people pass away when food was scarce and the old ones could no longer contribute any real help in procuring food and other necessities. Although the old people were well aware of that fact and accepted it as something unavoidable, they would naturally hang on to life as long as possible.

This is the story of one old Alaskan Indian woman, whom everybody called "Blind Maggie." The date of her birth was not known, but it was pretty well established that she was in her nineties. I knew her for several years when I mined in Chisana. Her son, Tiko, hunted and sold meat to the miners.

I prefer to call her "Lucky Maggie" because she really was lucky. In those days it wasn't always the easiest thing in the world for the natives in Alaska to get by. Food and clothing were hard to come by at times and when a member of a family got too old and feeble to do anything toward keeping the food supply in stock, they often got

116

lost somehow, never to be found again. Many attempts were made to leave Blind Maggie behind for good, but she was too lucky.

The first time they left her behind she was with her son, Tiko, his wife and children and some other natives, mostly relatives. They had a bunch of dogs along, for they were on a sheep hunting trip at the headwaters of Platinum Creek, a tributary of the Nabesna River. Maggie was about 98 years old at the time. Food had been very scarce, the fur had been poisoned by white trappers, and it was hard times for the natives. So it was agreed among the bunch that as Blind Maggie was useless and as she had already lived more than her full span of life, they would sneak off and leave her. They knew that she would never be able to find her way alone, being blind as a bat, and especially having to cross the big river to where the village was located. As she was also very hard of hearing it was easy to sneak off since they always kept her by herself in a little old five by seven tent.

One morning, about 4 a.m., the party left very quietly. Poor old Maggie woke up and discovered that she was alone. She knew why, but she wasn't about to give up. As blind as she was, she was still familiar with the country. She knew just where she was, and she knew it would take her at least three or four days to get to the village. She was plenty strong enough to do the walking, but she had to feel her way along the trail.

She rolled up her little tent, put it on her back with her blanket and started down stream, following the pack trail, slowly feeling her way to be sure she didn't get off the trail. It was sixteen miles to the village, and that day she made six miles. Then she covered herself with her light blanket, spread the little tent right over her and went to sleep.

The rest of the party got to the village but they failed to reckon what a dog will do when it misses a good friend. Maggie had made a pet of a little dog named Kuyon, apparently it was the only friend left in her worn-out life. That night Kuyon managed to slip his collar over his head and take off on the Platinum Creek Trail to look for his dear friend. Maggie awoke during the night with Kuyon barking and jumping all over her, and then she knew she would make it back home.

She still had a small piece of dried meat and some dried salmon which she shared with Kuyon and then she tied a small rope around his neck, left the little tent hanging in a tree, and Kuyon brought her into the village late that night.

The rest of the tribe explained to her that they had brought home a heavy load of meat and that two young boys were supposed to go and bring her back the next day. When Maggie asked them why they didn't tell her, they said, "We did, but maybe you didn't hear. Your hearing is getting very bad, Grandma."

Two years later they lived in Chisana, a small placer mining camp near the headwaters of the Chisana River. From there they took her on a similar trip into the Beaver Creek Valley and once again they left her behind, at least twenty-five miles from their home cabin. This time they made sure that she didn't have anything to eat and they disposed of Kuyon. But Maggie's luck still held. The pack trail through the Beaver Valley was a well-beaten horse trail and easy to follow. As soon as Maggie felt the sun the next morning she knew which way to go with the sun in back of her and by noon she had made almost five miles.

She lay down to rest for an hour while the sun was

nice and warm. She was about to start walking again when Jim Rogers, a prospector with a big pack on his back, caught up with her.

After she explained to him what had happened, he said, "Well, I'll be goddamned. Do you mean to tell me that they left you the hell and gone out here to die on the trail?"

Maggie said, "Oh, me old. No more good. Soon me die too. Much trouble, me."

"Oh, hell no," said Jim, "you are no trouble. I'll stay with you old, gal. Don't you worry. There is plenty of food in my pack. I'll bring you home and I really ought to kill all the other goddamn sons of bitches!"

Maggie said, "No, no, no! My people good people. No kill. Please no kill. If you like, better you kill me."

"Oh, for Christ's sake," said Jim. "Let's forget it. Sit down, old gal. I'll get us something to eat." And after a couple of sandwiches and several cups of tea, old Maggie could walk almost as fast as Jim, by hanging onto a small rope tied to his packboard. They made it in·less than three days.

Old Maggie was well fed and stronger than ever when she got back to Chisana where she had her own little bit of a cabin. Jim had promised the old gal that he wouldn't say anything to her relatives. So all he said was. "Here is your old Grandma. You shouldn't leave her so far behind." But to the miners around town he said, "We ought to hang some of them goddman bastards."

But it was soon forgotten. Old Maggie settled down in her little eight by twelve log cabin and lived on what scraps they gave her. She usually had a few dried salmon in her cabin and the miners gave her food and clothing until some-

119

body discovered that her relatives took it all away from her.

That winter it was noted that she was not properly clothed. So we made up a small sum of money and sent to Sears for a lot of good clothes for her which were to be given to her as a Christmas present. One Sidney Johnstone was appointed to deliver the present to her and at the same time give the rest of the tribe some instructions. We all knew that Johnstone was the man best suited for that purpose. So on Christmas day, Johnstone went over to the Indian settlement with a big package under his arm. He called them all outside and he said, as loud as he could raise his voice, "I have a package which is a Christmas present for old Blind Maggie and I want you all to come to her little cabin to witness what I give her."

They all followed him and when he got to her cabin he hollered to Maggie, saying, "Merry Christmas to you, Maggie. I am bringing you a Christmas present from all the miners in Chisana."

He unwrapped it and handed the contents to her one piece at a time. His loud voice could be heard a thousand yards away.

"Here is a suit of wool underwear, four pairs of wool stockings, one pair of overshoes, two pairs of woolen mitts, one pair of leather mitts, four pairs of woolen gloves, and here are some dresses, a heavy sweater, four white sheets, one pillow, six pillowcases, four woolen blankets and one down-filled quilt. One pair of house slippers and a big box full of cookies and cake."

Then he turned around and faced the bunch of Indians and shouted as loud as he could, "Now if I ever catch any of you wearing any of the clothes belonging to Maggie, I'll kill every goddamn one of you!"

120

It really must have hit the spot because not one piece of any of her clothing or blankets was taken from her. She was well dressed that winter and we all made sure that she had wood to burn in her little air-tight heater, and that she always had some food on her little corner shelf. Although she didn't eat much, in the spring she looked better than she had for many years.

They made one more try that summer, but this time, instead of taking her out any place, they decided to leave her alone right in her little cabin. This time they depended on nature to take its course.

Everybody had left town. All the miners were busy on their claims, most of them about ten miles distant from Chisana. Every one of the Indians had just got over a terrible cold and finally old Maggie caught it. They quietly left town. Before they left they emptied all the water buckets, including Maggie's. It was about 300 yeards out to the creek bank. She was around a hundred years old then and she was the only person in town and down with a bad cold.

A small plane landed on the field the second day after they had all left. It was heard and seen by most people in the area but to this day it remains a mystery plane. But whoever it was, there must have been either a doctor or nurse, or both, aboard it, because about a week later one of the miners came down to check on old Maggie. He found the cabin cleaned as it had never been cleaned before. There was cold medicine, aspirin tablets, vitamin pills, two boxes of Kleenex tissues, two full buckets of water, and a smell of disinfectant.

Maggie was sitting on a block of wood, which was her only furniture, chewing on a piece of dried moose meat. When he asked her how she was, she said, "Oh me good.

121

Nice white people come from plane. Stay two days. Make me feel good. Take care me. Wash me just like baby. Give me medicine, too. Me feel like long time ago."

She had a smile on her face that nobody had ever seen before. Not only that, but she wore that smile for almost seven years more. They gave up trying to lose her as it seemed that she always came out of it in better condition than she had been in before. Also, Maggie had made up her mind not to leave her little cabin in Chisana any more. They figured she was 106 years old when she died in her sleep, in her own bed. I didn't see her then, but those who did said she still had that same mysterious smile on her face.

CHAPTER TWENTY-NINE

THE LONG AERIAL

In the early 1930's throughout the lonely places of Alaska a good radio made the winter months a whole lot more cheerful.

Everybody had their own peculiar idea about how to put up a good aerial in order to get the best reception and far-away stations. Some of them said a real high aerial was the best. Others said that the height didn't make any difference but the aerial had to be put up in a square so as to receive from all directions.

But there was one man by the name of George Harris who was all for long aerials. "The longer it is," he said, "the more stations you'll pick up and the better results you'll get." It was almost a religion with him. He made it a point to tell everybody about it. He wrote letters to his friends and called them on the telephone and told them by all means put up a long aerial if they had the wire. If they didn't have the wire he would often get hold of some, bring it, and help them put it up. It was admitted by all whom he persuaded to lengthen their aerials that they did get much better reception.

Several times he stayed overnight with me in my cabin when I lived at Slana, which is where a forty mile stretch of graveled road branches off from the main highway to the Nabesna gold mine. The mine was closed when World War II broke out, but they left a watchman in camp to look after everything. The telephone from Slana was abandoned when the government put up the new telephone line along the main highway, but the mine watchman and I were the only ones left on the old forty-mile line. We talked to each other almost every day about the news we heard on the radio as well as the local news.

One day I got a letter from George telling me that he had added an extension to his already very long aerial and oh! what wonderful reception he was getting. He said he would be up to see me soon and maybe stay at my place a couple of days and help me put up an extension to my aerial which he had told me so many times "was way too short!"

Finishing his letter he said, "My aerial is almost one-half mile long now." The mention of one-half mile was what set me to thinking about the forty mile telephone line to Nabesna. It was only a two-man telephone anyway. Why not hook onto it and really have a long aerial?

I called the watchman and told him what I had in mind and he agreed with me that it might be a good idea. So we both hooked our aerials onto it. Oh boy, what a difference! Believe me, we really found out that a long aerial was worthwhile.

So I wrote a letter to George and told him to come on up for a visit but not to bring any wire along as I had already extended my aerial and was getting all kinds of stations all over the world. I didn't have long to wait. As soon as George got my letter he came tearing up to my place in his old Ford coupe. It was dark when he got to my place but I had a hunch it was him when I saw the lights in front of my cabin. I turned on the radio and as I had just put in a brand new 1000 hour battery, the finest kind of music came to George's ears as soon as he turned off his car.

When he came in he said, "Now you have done something worthwhile, Knut. That's what I have been trying to tell you for years but you would never listen to me."

After we had a couple of beers and a meal, George got in front of that radio and turned the dial and it was so loaded with stations that in several places they couldn't be separated.

"By golly," said George, "this beats anything I've seen yet. How long is your aerial?"

I said, "Oh, a little over forty miles."

He gave me a funny look. "No kidding, " he said, "how much did you add to it?"

"I told you forty miles."

He went out with his flashlight but he couldn't spot the place where I had spliced onto the telephone line.

"Wait 'til morning," he said. "I'll find out."

Which, of course, he did.

Then he said, "Well, it goes to show that I am right about getting better results with long aerials. You get better reception here than anybody I know of. But for a little while, Knut, I actually thought you were a little off your rocker when you insisted that you had a forty mile aerial. Well, I've helped a lot of people put extensions on their aerials but I can't very well go around and add that much to them. But I can at least tell them that if they want to see what a long aerial will do for them, go up to Slana and see Knut Peterson."

CHAPTER THIRTY

TELEPHONE REPAIRMEN

Now that I just got through telling about the long aerial I had better tell about when we had a break in that same telephone line.

As I have already mentioned, it was forty miles long. I lived at one end of it and Harry Boyden, the watchman, lived at the mine which was the other end of it.

Harry, of course, wanted to get all the news and gossip from down along the main road as he was the only white man up there. The only way he could get it was to call me. So he spliced the wire whenever a moose happened to walk into it and break it, which happened because it was strung on tripods. A big animal would rub itself against the tripod poles and tip them over, leaving the wire on the ground.

One winter Harry had been trying to call for several days and realized the wire was broken. He knew I was home because if I left for any length of time I always called him and told him where I was going and about when

126

I would be back. I also knew that there was something wrong as I had been trying to get him, too.

So Harry hired an Indian known as Nabesna John to go down to Slana with his dog team, mail a bunch of letters for him and at the same time keep an eye on the telephone line on the way down. He was to fix the break, wherever it was, and then bring Harry's mail on his return trip. Harry gave him a piece of telephone wire to make the splice with, and pliers and a wire cutter. But the next morning John took off and forgot to put all the repair tools and wire in his sled. After he had made fifteen miles he found the break and stopped and fixed it.

The next day John came to my place. It had been heavy going and he was tired—so were his dogs. I was glad to see him as I had been wondering about Boyden. John stayed at my place a couple of days to rest up and, of course, when he told me he had fixed the line I kept trying to call Harry—but no answer!

I asked John, "Are you sure there was no other break in that line?"

"No more break," he said. "Just one I see and fix. All the way I watch line but no more break."

"Well," I said, "there is something wrong some place. Maybe moose walk through again so be sure to watch close on the way back, John. In the meantime, I'll keep ringing."

After John had been gone a couple of days and I figured he was back home at Nabesna I was puzzled because I still couldn't get Harry. I got tired of ringing as the days went by and finally I got to where I would ring just once a day. I knew that Harry must be ringing on the other end, too.

Finally, about two weeks after John had left my place, Harry Boyden in person came to my place with his own dog team. He was about 67 years old and it was quite a trip for him. He was tired and in a bad mood. While he was unhooking his dogs I put the coffeepot on.

When he came in he said, "Wait till you hear this. You won't believe it."

I poured him half a cup of coffee and put in a good slug of 151 proof Hudson Bay Rum and then he went on to tell me the whole story.

"But listen to this now," he said. "When I came to where John said he had fixed it, what do you suppose I found?"

"Well," I said, "I have no idea. Maybe he didn't splice it very good and it came apart again."

Harry said, "No, that wasn't it. Here is what the damn fool done. He forgot the wire that I gave him to splice it with. When he found the break, damned if he didn't make a big eye, or loop, in each end of the wire and then tied a half-inch rope between the wire ends. He strung it up high as it would go with a forked pole, leaving a five foot gap between the two ends of wire. And that's how I found it after paying him $30 and a hundred pounds of cornmeal to make the trip for me!"

"But it was only fifteen miles from Nabesna where it was broken," I said. "How come you didn't go back home only fifteen miles instead of making twenty-five miles down here?"

"Well," he said, "after seeing how he fixed it and then not even telling me that he had been using rope, I didn't trust the twenty-five mile stretch so I decided to come on down."

CHAPTER THIIRTY-ONE

NEW MAN

It was in the fall or early part of the winter of 1916 that George Newman left with a winter outfit to do some winter prospecting on a creek about seventy miles from his base in Fairbanks. He hired a man with a big team of dogs to haul his supplies. When he got to his destination, the dog musher drove back to Fairbanks. Newman built a small cabin and proceeded to thaw the gravel and dig holes to bedrock in search of a paystreak.

There was a small Indian village about ten miles from his new location. He soon got well acquainted with the Indians, bought meat from them, and they always called him George; they didn't know his last name.

About the middle of the winter, another prospector moved in on a creek about ten miles on the opposite side of the village. He wasn't the friendly type, so the Indians stayed clear of him. Among themselves, they referred to him as the new man. One of the Indians had a trapline which passed close to his camp. He always looked for

129

smoke when he went by there with his dog team.

About the first of February, he came by the new man's camp for the third time in a week without seeing any smoke. When he went by with his dog team, he decided to investigate. To his horror, he found the new man dead. He was frozen stiff.

Soon, it was the main news in the little village. One of the young native boys had a long trapline toward Fairbanks. He shared a small stopover cabin with a white trapper about halfway. After the news of the white man's death, he left for that place, hoping to meet his white friend, which he did.

When he told about the death of the new man, the white man got all excited. He asked the native, "Are you sure it was Newman?"

"Yes, new man. Me no know him very good. Him dig holes. Look for gold. New man, that's all I know."

Everybody in Fairbanks knew Newman. All the miners, prospectors, and trappers out in the bush knew him. The white trapper took off for Fairbanks to notify the marshal. Two big dog teams were soon on the trail, headed for Newman's camp, carrying the marshal and a friend of Newman's. One of the mushers knew just where to go, since he had hauled Newman's outfit.

When they got close to the little cabin, smoke was pouring out of the stovepipe. Newman appeared in the door, a surprised look on his face. The marshal and his party were still more surprised. The marshal walked up to George, shook his hand, and said, "Why, George, you are alive!"

"Just what the hell made you think I wouldn't be?"

The marshal explained the confusion and they tried to figure out the reason. First they thought one of the natives had started a false rumor, but soon it was all cleared up. The marshal went with the native to pick up the new man, whose identity was still a mystery.

The sad news in the Fairbanks newspaper had spread all over the country, and for years George Newman kept meeting old friends who told him that he looked exactly like their old friend, George Newman.

CHAPTER THIRTY-TWO

WEATHER REPORT

In the 1920's, when fox trapping in Alaska brought big money, one trapper lived along the Old Eagle Trail, about twenty miles north of the Richardsen Highway. The old Signal Corps telephone line went right by his place, so he had a telephone in his main cabin.

One fall he killed two fat moose right by his cabin which of course was against the law. But he had a deal on with the trader at the highway. He was to bring a fat moose down to him with his dog team, and the trader would pay him thirty-five cents a pound.

In those days, everybody along the road would listen in as soon as they heard the telephone ring, so the trapper and trader had a code. If the trapper called and asked about the weather, that meant he had made a kill and was ready to come down with a load of meat. If there was no game warden at the trading post or in the neighborhood, the trader would say: "Oh, it's fine weather down here. Ten above zero." If the warden was in the neighborhood, he would say: "It's not too bad here, but I hear there is a cold wave on the way. It may hit here any time." If the warden was at the trading post with his dog team, he would say: "Gosh, it's cold down here. It's almost fifty below zero."

Everything worked out okay until there was only one load of meat left. It was a mild morning in December when the trapper called the trading post. The warden was there and stayed there overnight. He was sitting in the small dining room, drinking coffee. The trader was cooking breakfast and the phone was in the kitchen. He couldn't help hearing the phone ring and what was said. It went like this:

"Hello, yes, this is Herb. Oh, it's terrible cold down here. It's almost fifty below zero. I wouldn't start off, Jack, unless there is something you need real bad."

The warden went out to look at the thermometer. It read twelve above zero. When he came in, he said, "Say, Herb, you sure must have been sleepy when you looked at that thermometer this morning. I heard you tell Jack that it was fifty below."

Herb said, "Oh, gosh, my glasses must have been frosted. That's okay. I'll call him later and tell him."

The warden said. "You go ahead with breakfast, Herb. I will call him. I haven't talked to Jack since last September." He rang two long and three short. "Hello, Jack, this is Nelson, the game warden. How goes it?"

"Oh, just fine."

"Say, Jack, Herb gave you a bad report on the weather I think he was still sleeping when he looked. It's only twelve above here."

After a few minutes of conversation, the warden said, "Well, if I don't see you before, I'll see you in the spring."

After breakfast the warden left. Herb called back again

and said, "It's warming to beat hell now. I kind of think it will stay warm for a few days, so it may be a good idea for you to come on down. You know how the weather seems to change fast sometimes."

Jack said, "Okay. I'll make this trip. But after that I don't give a damn about the weather any more."

That evening, Herb got several calls from the road-houses along the Richardsen. They all had the same question.

"Say, Herb, what kind of damn thermometer have you got over there?"

Herb said, "To tell the truth, it has been acting funny for some time, but I got some new ones now. I am going to give Jack one of them, so he don't need to ask about the temperature no more. You guys can quit listening in now. There will be no more weather news from here."

CHAPTER THIRTY-THREE

TWO MEN IN A BLIZZARD

It was sometime in the 1920's when the roads, what few there were in Alaska, were only about the width of a car or truck. In many places, you had to pick a favorable place if you met another car in order to get by each other, and if you got caught in a snowstorm, you had to be a good driver just to stay on the road.

One fall when the road crew shut down the work, they were short a driver to bring all the Model A dump trucks into Chitina, which at that time was the headquarters of the Alaska Road Commission. So two old-timers who had worked on the gravel crew all summer, mostly with a number two shovel, volunteered to drive the extra truck. Gus and Bill could move a truck, and that was about all. By no means did they have enough experience to drive anything on the road.

In those days, there was no traffic in the fall of the year anyway, so the foreman said okay. They insisted on being the last truck, saying that they wanted to drive slow.

135

So they started out.

Years before, whoever had put up the mileposts had made a mistake. After they put up milepost twenty-five, they had simply measured off another mile and put up the next post and marked it mile twenty-five. It had never been corrected.

Gus and Bill drove the old truck real slow for about thirty miles, and then a blinding snowstorm hit. It was next to impossible to see the road, and every few minutes they had to stop to clean the windshield. Instead of getting better, the storm got worse, and they finally slid off the narrow road and into the ditch.

They tried for quite a while to get back on it again, but it was no go. So they said, "To hell with it. We'll walk and leave the damn truck sit here in the ditch."

So they started walking. The wind was smack in their faces, but they knew there was a roadhouse at mile sixteen. After they had walked about a mile bucking snow and wind, Bill spotted a milepost and they both walked over to it.

"Oh, well," they said, "this is mile twenty-five. We'll make the roadhouse about dark."

They had to talk loud to be heard above the wind. They started off again, heads down and wiping snow off their faces. At times it blew so hard that it almost stopped them, and they were on the verge of turning back.

Finally they spotted another milepost. They both walked right over to it and there it was, staring them right in the face, plain as could be: Mile Twenty-Five!

They both looked at it a few moments and then Gus wiped the snow off his face, looked at Bill and shouted, "Well, goddammit! We are holding our own, anyway!"

The foreman hadn't forgotten about them. After

walking less than another mile, he met them, and behind him was a young fellow with his model A truck. They found a place nearby to turn around. The other Model A was left in the ditch all winter. After they got to the road-house and had something to eat, the foreman asked them, "What would you fellows have done if you hadn't made it to this place and I hadn't come out to look for you?"

Gus said, "Oh, I suppose we would have camped out there some place at mile twenty-five."

CHAPTER THIRTY-FOUR

STUCK IN THE MUD

In the early 1920's the U.S. Army Signal Corps had their way stations scattered along the old Eagle trail from Valdez to Eagle on the bank of the Yukon River.

The largest part of that trail was just a pack trail for horses in the summertime and dog teams in the winter along the telephone line. The heavy freight was brought to Eagle by river boat, and the mail came through once a month from Valdez. A lot of freight was brought to the way stations from Valdez by horse team and wagons, over a narrow, partly graveled road.

Some of the trading posts had small trucks by then and hauled their supplies as far as the road was built. In dry weather everything was fine, but when it rained heavily, they had lots of trouble.

Then the army got some flat-bed trucks and hauled their supplies from Valdez as far as they could, and freighted the supplies by pack horses along the trail for the way stations. The army usually sent two men with each truck besides the driver, so that if they got stuck, the driver would have some help. They also carried tents, stove, saws and axes and plenty of extra clothes and bedding so that if they couldn't get out, they could set up camp until they got more help. Of course, they also had plenty of groceries along, and they carried a telephone they could hook onto the line anywhere and call Valdez for help. The help usually consisted of a team of horses or another truck and several men.

Earl Hirst, a trader, was on his way home from Valdez with a small truck and a load of supplies for his place of business when he came to where an army truck was badly stuck. It had skidded into the ditch with both wheels on the right side. There wasn't enough room left on the narrow road for Earl to get by, so he walked over to the tent the soldiers had set up near the road, but there was nobody there. A pot of coffee was simmering on the stove, so he sat down on a block of wood and drank a cupful.

In a few minutes the boys came into camp with a .22 rifle and six spruce hens. When they found out that Earl couldn't get by, one of them said, "Oh, Christ, we didn't get out far enough. We're blocking the road."

So they got their saws and axes and cut some trees to build up the side of the road. Earl got by without any trouble.

He stopped and walked back to the boys and said, "Well, you're not stuck too bad. If we dig a little in front of the wheels, I'll pull you out."

One of the boys, a corporal, spoke up and said, "No, I'll be goddamned if you will. We got lots of time to get out."

The other two added, "Christ, yes! We've got three years to get out. We signed up for three years and not only that, we just found out a few minutes ago that there are lots of Dolly Varden trout in that little stream over there about a thousand yards from here. We also discovered that our hook-on telephone is out of order, so there is no way we can get word to Valdez to let them know that we're in trouble. It will be at least four days before they'll decide to come and look for us unless some damn nuthead happens to pass by here on the way to Valdez and squeals on us when they get there. Anyway, we're glad we got it fixed now so other trucks can get by. But for Christ's sake, don't tell anybody that we're here."

Earl said, "Okay, boys. I didn't even see you." And he drove on home.

A week later somebody told Earl there were three trucks parked there and another tent had been set up. They said they could smell fried fish half a mile before you got to their camp.

Not a bad place to be stuck in the mud!

CHAPTER THIRTY-FIVE

DEEP FREEZE

Three of us were prospecting together on the Lower Beaver Creek, close to the Canadian line, one winter in the 1930's. It had been real nice going. Then about the middle of January, I took my five husky malemutes and went to Chisana for some supplies. I got the supplies and stayed one night at King City on the Chisana River. The next night I stayed at Garden Creek Cabin. From there I could make it in about four hours through a low, flat pass to our cabin on the Beaver, where my brother and a fellow by the name of Pete Ekland were waiting for me.

But something went wrong that day. It was a little windy when I left that morning, and the wind got stronger and stronger. I had a light load and was making good time until the snow started drifting in the trail. Before I was halfway, it was blowing so hard that I could hardly see the lead dog for drifting snow. We were facing right into it, and for a while I thought about turning back. But we kept plugging along until it got so smoky with fine drifting snow, it was almost impossible to keep my eyes open.

The dogs worked hard, knowing that they were headed for the home cabin. I knew that somewhere not too far from our trail there was a cabin on the Canadian side that belonged to a Canadian Indian trapper, but I wasn't about to look for it in that kind of weather. There were scattered spruce trees most of the way, and in a few spots fairly thick clumps of spruce. I kept looking for one of those clumps of timber, intending to unhook the team and make some sort of a shelter.

I stopped the team and sat down on the nose of the sled to rest, and all five dogs lay down. I couldn't see any sign of the trail, but I saw a blaze right in front of me, so I knew we must still be on it.

All of a sudden the five dogs got together as if somebody had pulled a switch and had given them an electric shock. First I thought there was a moose close by. I wasn't sure what it was, but the way they all got together and turned their heads to the left, they had heard something that I couldn't hear above the howling wind.

Fritz, the lead dog, looked back at me as if to tell me, "Let us go that way."

Just on impulse, I decided to let him go anywhere he wanted to. We were in a bad blizzard, and there didn't seem to be much difference which direction we took. So I said, "Okay, Fritz, come haw. It's all yours."

All five of them took off like a bunch of scared wolves. The snow wasn't very deep or they couldn't have done it. The ground was rough, and I almost tipped over several times. I was riding, and the wind hit us from the side.

In about ten minutes, I stopped them again. I had to apply the brake this time.

Now I could hear it—dogs barking! We must be headed for the Canadian Indian's cabin. Good deal! Anything to get out of that terrible wind and blowing snow. It wasn't very cold, only about five below zero. The trees began to be more plentiful, and in a few more minutes we were in heavy timber. Then I saw snowshoe tracks and a moment later, there was the cabin. Indian, dogs, and everything!

I ran the nose of the sled against a tree and walked up and talked to the cabin's occupant. He was a very nice man.

"Glad to see you," he said. "My name is Eno. Tie your dogs any place. Soon we have hot tea. You stay here with me maybe three days, maybe four days. Long time wind blow this time."

"How do you know?" I asked.

He said, "I don't know how, but I just know. That's all."

And, by golly, he did. It blew as I had never seen it blow for almost five days. Of course, I'll always be grateful to Eno. We put in four days together, and the wind was almost tearing his log cabin apart. It broke off big spruce trees. It was a terrible storm.

I had depended on getting home to our cabin on the Beaver, so I didn't have any dog food. But Eno gave me meat, and I gave him sugar, tea, beans, tobacco and other things that he needed. By the third day, it looked to me like there was nothing left for his own dogs, let alone feeding mine.

"Don't worry," Eno said. "If big wind blow one month, me eat, you eat, dog eat."

He had predicted the wind and I took his word for it. On the morning of the fourth day, Eno got up early.

"Today," he said, "you and me work."

143

"Okay," I said. "I'll be glad to do something."

About fifty feet from his cabin was a nice clear spring stream, and I had noticed a dome-shaped knoll right close to the water's edge. It looked like a small haystack or a big beaver house. Eno led the way over to it with a pick, two good axes, and a shovel.

We went to work on the dome-shaped knoll, picking, cutting and shoveling a layer of moss, then a layer of ice, another layer of moss, and a layer of ice, until we finally broke through to dry, white snow. From that dry snow Eno pulled out a quarter of the fattest moose meat I've ever seen.

"Three years ago," he explained, "I cache them two fat cow moose here. I got big family. But that time I got lots of fat moose meat. That winter not many moose. I need meat. I dig out."

I had never seen anything like that before. Here was the finest kind of meat that had been killed three years before and frozen hard as flint in that dome-shaped knoll that I thought looked out of place.

I found out from Eno how he had built his freezer. First, he laid the floor. With the open spring stream, which never froze regardless of how cold it got, and using a big wash tub, he mixed snow and water into a thick slush and spread it on the moss-covered ground to freeze until the floor was more than two feet thick. Then he hauled the meat, stacked it on the ice floor, and covered it with dry snow. The meat, of course, was frozen hard as a rock. After that, he worked about a week mixing snow slush and freezing on layers of ice, hauling moss to cover the ice, and then adding more layers of ice.

It must have been a big job. But oh, what a deep freeze that was! I guess we can call that "man-made permafrost."

We had a nice, big, fat T-bone steak for supper that night, and fed our dogs some meat that made them wag their tails. I left for Beaver Creek the next day. It was still blowing some, but I had a well-rested and well-fed team of dogs, thanks to Eno! I am afraid I would have been in a bad fix if I hadn't come into his place. I am still thankful to the keen hearing of a team of young malemute dogs and my sudden decision to let them go wherever they wanted to go.

CHAPTER THIRTY-SIX

CALLING ALL WOLVES

"Calling all wolves" must be what the wolf is broadcasting when food is scarce and small game hunting is not sufficient to nourish his hundred to two-hundred-pound frame. I often wondered how wolves get together in large packs. Then one winter evening in the 1930's, I was trapping along the Chisana River and I found out.

My main camp was a small cabin located at a place where the river comes out of the high mountains and cuts through a big flat on its way to join the Tanana River. It was within hearing distance of that cabin that the "calling all wolves" started on a hillside about two or three miles away. I was reading one evening, when all of a sudden I heard the long-drawn mournful howl, and it sounded as if it was just a few yards away. I got busy planning to set a couple of traps on the river, as the mournful howl went on and on with monotonous regularity all night. Next morning I set out two traps on the river bar and scattered scent around them.

The second evening the same call in the same direction started at dusk. About 8 o'clock that evening I heard another howl way off in the distance somewhere. And before I went to bed I could hear a couple more in another direction. I thought that within a short time I would have one or all of them in my traps. But the howling went on and on for over a week, and it came from all directions. As a rule I had a team of dogs when I was out like that, but that winter I was alone. My brother had our team and was trapping in other parts.

For the fifth night, I wish that I could have had a tape recorder. You talk about howling. I had never, and I am sure I never will again hear anything like it. Besides that it was Christmas Eve. Silent night, holy night, I thought to myself. The wolves must be planning on a big Christmas party.

At the time I had been in Alaska sixteen years. I had seen and heard wolf packs many times, and I had trapped a lot of them, but I had never seen or heard anything like this. More than thirty years later, I am still here and I have never again seen anything like it, and I am sure I never will. If I hadn't witnessed this with my own eyes and ears I wouldn't have believed it. For four days the howling got louder and louder. It was actually one continuous mournful howl sounding like it was moving around in a big circle on an enormous merry-go-round, getting smaller, closing into wherever the center happened to be.

I didn't then and I still don't believe that a wolf or a pack of wolves will attack and kill a human being. But I did have an uneasy feeling. I had several traps out for lynx, but the short days, cold weather, Christmas holidays and New Year's, and the country loaded with howling wolves, gave ample excuse for staying right close to my little cabin.

It was either the first or second of January that the howling sounded as if it was running out of power, getting fainter and weaker. I wondered if they were getting together or farther away. Then all of a sudden it was quiet.

The next couple of days I checked my lynx sets. The third day I was across the river and on my way back. It was beginning to get dark when I got to the river. I had two lynx on a small hand sled. I was tired and glad to be close to home. It was about a mile across the river to my cabin.

Just as I came out of the woods and glanced out on the open river bar, I got the surprise of my life. The snow was beaten down as if a herd of five or six hundred caribou had traveled down stream. Then I looked down river and there they were, about three fourths of a mile away, disappearing into a wooded and brushy island. How many had already gone in I'll never know. But there were at least a hundred wolves loping along steadily, the pack gradually getting smaller as they disappeared into the island. I carried a .22 rifle and I fired a couple of shots in the air to see if it would excite them. Maybe they didn't even hear it; anyway, it didn't have any effect on them.

If I had come to the river a few minutes before, I would have been right alongside of them. And I have often wondered just what I would have done when all of a sudden a couple of hundred wolves would have been within ten yards of me, slowly moving down stream as I was coming out of the woods onto the river bar, or if they had decided to follow my trail. I am sure the first thing I would have done as soon as I had spotted them was get a fire going under a big spruce tree. There were a lot of good sized trees along that trail, and there are always dry needles close to the trunk. I always carried a tobacco can full of sawdust soaked with kerosene, and lots of matches. With that I would have had a fire going in less than a minute. But regardless of the number of hungry wolves, I think they would have left the trail as soon as they saw me and walked through the woods.

I've caught a lot of wolves and I've seen packs of wolves many times. The wolf stays clear of man. I've read hair-raising accounts of men who claimed to have been surrounded by wolves, and banged away at them, saving one last shell for themselves, but somehow they always lived through it.

The day after I saw the big pack, I went upstream following the wide, hard-packed trail they had made. When I got to my frist trap, there were three wolf toes in it. The rest of it had been torn to pieces and eaten right there. There were a few spots of bloody snow and pieces of skin and bones. The next set had a whole foot in it, but the wolf had been eaten like the other one.

About four miles upstream from my cabin the beaten trail entered the river bar from the foothills. I followed the beaten path along the foothills for five miles and found a place where a small bull moose had been killed and eaten. A few bones, the head, a few strips of hide were scattered around over a wide area.

I wanted to go farther, but the days were short and it was time to hit for home. I carried my 30-06 on that trip. I would have liked to follow their trail where they had come together, and see the many trails leading in from all directions. Before I got around to it about a foot of snow fell.

I know a lot of you won't believe this, but regardless of whether or not you do, the facts remain the same. You never saw anybody in the hospital, badly torn up by a wolf or wolves, and you never will. The bear is quite different, as I found out the hard way. But don't worry about the wolf; he is scared of you whether he is alone or in a pack.

CHAPTER THIRTY-SEVEN

TIMBER RABBITS

When I was mining in Chisana, a small placer mining camp near the head of the Chisana River in the 1930's, the price of gold was on the way up from $20 to $30 per ounce and the little mined-out camp had a small stampede. Every few days some new man would show up, introduce himself, and ask where he could find some gold.

In the fall we all moved down to what we referred to as the town of Chisana, about ten miles below the mining claims. There we had our winter cabins and there was a small landing strip and mail was brought in once a month. Most of us took off for the trapline in the winter with our dog teams as at that time fur brought good prices.

One fall, Pete Ekland, a miner, and I were sitting around waiting for snow. A boy about 20 years old came in on the mail plane. He was from Montana, and when he heard they'd raised the price of gold, he decided to go to Alaska and do some mining. Pete had a big cabin so he let the kid stay there with him. In a day or so Pete came over to my cabin and told me that at last a man had come to Chisana who knew all about mining, prospecting, hunting, fishng, and trapping.

"Come on over this evening," he said, "and we'll have some fun."

Pete was full of hell and the kid was full of bull, so I looked for some entertainment. The kid's name was Ben Muller. After a big supper of roasted moose meat and rice we settled down to talk and I noticed that Ben had us all beat. The kid could talk—and I am sure he could talk faster than he could think! He told us about some of the creeks he had mined in Montana, also trapping and hunting and many other things. Once in a while Pete would ask something like, "And how long did you mine there?" and "How many years did you trap in western Montana?" And so on.

The talk finally drifted around to dog teams and Ben said that when he trapped along the foothills of the Rocky Mountains he had a team of nine dogs. Pete asked him how long a trapline he had. He said, "Four hundred miles."

"And how many miles could you make a day on an average?"

"Oh, about sixty or seventy miles."

Pete winked at me as he said to Ben, "You must have had old work dogs."

Ben said, "No, they were young dogs."

"Oh, they couldn't have been, " said Pete, "or you surely wouldn't be all day making sixty or seventy miles."

"Well," Ben said, "I usually came in early picking up my fur along the trail, resetting my traps and when I got to my stopping camp I had a load of fur to skin."

Pete said, "Oh, that's right, excuse me, I forgot all about trapping. Yes, I see now that was fairly good. No doubt if you just took off for a trip you would make a lot more than sixty miles with nine dogs."

Ben said, "Oh, Christ, yes. My trapline was seven hundred miles from home and I usually made that trip in two days."

When Pete asked him about hauling out his big load of fur he said, "Oh, the fur buyers always came in to my trapline at the end of the season with big teams and bought my fur for cash money."

Ben had a ready answer to anything we asked him. Pete and I figured it out the next day—according to all the places he had been and the length of time at each place he had to be way past fifty years old.

Horesefelt on the upper Beaver Creek is about forty miles from Chisana and when Ben found out from Pete that there was nobody trapping there and that there was a good cabin he decided to go there and clean up some fur.

"But there is no snow," Pete said, "and you haven't got any dogs or sled to get your outfit over there."

"Oh, hell," replied Ben, "I won't need much of an outfit, and a mere forty miles—I'll be over there in a few hours, so I'll just go over there and scout around to see if there is plenty of fur. You say there is lots of sheep on the hills so I don't need to bring much food."

Pete had told him where he could find some traps not far from the cabin so he took off on the well-beaten Horsefelt trail saying, "Well, boys, if I get into a good showing of fur I may not be back for three or four months." But Ben was back in ten days, tired, disappointed and almost starved.

"But how could you go hungry," Pete asked, "with all the sheep over there?"

"Oh, hell," said Ben, "I could never get close enough

153

to them."

Pete said, "Why didn't you kill one of the timber rabbits? Nobody ever goes hungry at Horsefelt with all them timber rabbits below the cabin."

"What do you mean—timber rabbits? I never heard of them."

Pete said, "No, I guess you haven't got any out in Montana. Too bad I forgot to mention it to you before you left. I never thought of it."

Ben was getting interested all over again. "What about them," he said, "are they different from ordinary rabbits?"

"Oh, there is no comparison," said Pete, "you need a big gun to kill a timber rabbit."

"How big are they?" Ben asked.

"Oh, about 200 pounds and there is lots of them down below the Horsefelt cabin in the big timber. They can jump almost a hundred feet—they are not scared of anything, easy to kill and good eating."

Then I asked Pete about the high bench right close to where he said the rabbits were. "Isn't there a lot of native potatoes up there too, Pete?"

"Oh, you mean the siwash spuds! Oh, hell yes, and they are much better than any spuds you can buy and there is a lot of wild onions too, but they may be froze now. I doubt if you can dig them in a couple of days."

Ben was all excited and ready to go again but he took a big load of food along on that trip. It was a freaky fall. We didn't get any snow until about the first of December and we lost the best part of the trapping season. Before we left Chisana a man from the Canadian side whom we knew showed up. He often came to Chisana and bought a few groceries from the trader there. He had stayed overnight in

154

the Horsefelt cabin and he said, "There is a young boy staying in the Horsefelt cabin and he is off his rocker. He is hunting below the cabin amongst the big spruce trees for what he calls timber rabbits. When he told me what they were like I knew damn well he was crazy, and besides that he has been up on the high bench looking for spuds and onion." So Pete and I told him about Ben.

We never did see the young trapper again. When the snow came we left for our trapline but when we came back to Chisana about the first of January, old man N. P. Nelson, old miner and discoverer of the Chisana placer gold, said the kid had come out. He said, "He wore me out with his long line of bull 'til I decided to hand him some. He told me," said Nelson, "that you two were pretty nice guys but awful damn liars. I told him, 'Well now, Ben, I wouldn't say that. I know them two to be reliable men and I always depend on what they tell me. How old are you, Ben?' He told me, 'I'll be 21 in April.'"

Nelson went on with his story—"Yes, I told him, 'I thought so. You see, Ben, this is pretty far north and no doubt you are magnetic. I suppose you know there are a few people who are magnetic until they are past twenty-five years of age.' Ben told me that he knew that but he didn't have any idea that he was one of them. 'But you must be, Ben,' I said, 'because if you hunted for timber rabbit below the Horsefelt cabin and didn't see any, that in itself is ample proof that you are a magnetic. Any person who happens to be a magnetic and makes a move toward the North Pole as far as you did usually gets afflicted pretty bad. There is no doubt but what you walked right amongst the timber rabbits and looked right at them with eyes so magnetized that the rabbits appeared to be willow bushes

155

or something. You are lucky you didn't walk into the Lady Springs and drown.' 'Where is the Lady Springs?' Ben wanted to know. I told him they are spotted all through the woods below the Horsefelt cabin where he was hunting. Most people are scared to go through there after dark."

The next day Ben told Nelson he was afraid that he was so heavy magnetized that he might go crazy, but Nelson said, "Oh, no, Ben, I've never heard of anybody going bughouse. Of course they do get a little funny. When you get back to Montana you'll be as normal as anybody else." Ben left on the next plane.

During the time Nelson was telling all this we drank about a fifth of Hudson Bay Rum. As Nelson mixed the last drink he said, "It's a good thing we're out of rum, boys, or we would all be magnetized."

Pete said, "Yes, and maybe rabbitized too."

"And besides that," I added, "we would most likely fall into the Lady Springs and drown."

CHAPTER THIRTY-EIGHT

LONGEVITY

One old sourdough who lived alone in a small cabin near the Yukon River was known to be 104 years old and in surprisingly good health at the time a news reporter was sent out to interview him concerning his longevity. The reporter was told by neighbors that the old boy was a pretty good plug, but at times very cranky and a hard man to talk to because he never stopped talking long enough for anyone else to get a word in.

It was late in the afternoon and almost dark when the reporter came to his cabin and introduced himself. Asked to what he attributed his long life and excellent health the old sourdough said, "I've been too goddamn busy to even give it a thought. Hell, it's almost dark now and I haven't even got my wood in for the night, and the gas lamp is empty. I've got bread in the oven due to come out in ten minutes. I've been washing clothes and they are not rinsed out yet. I still have to make two trips to the creek for water. I can't find my goddamn flashlight. I wouldn't be surprised but what George forgot to bring it back, and now the damn dog is beginning to yap about his supper as if I had nothing to do but look after him. Oh, Christ! I can smell the bread almost burning." He opened the oven door and out came two delicious smelling golden brown loaves of bread.

The reporter started to say something but the old man still held the floor and kept right on. "It looks like rain," he said, "and I didn't get that leak in the roof fixed yet. Oh, hell, it will have to leak in the bucket tonight. I'll fix it tomorrow. I can't stand to listen to the goddamn drip, drip, drip. I am going to cut some moose ribs and put on a stew. Why don't you lie down in that extra bed over there and take a rest. The stew should be done in about three hours. I am going out now to fill the lamp and as dark as it is, I'll spill more gas than I'll get in the tank. Why the hell don't George buy himself a flashlight instead of borrowing mine all the time. This will be the last goddamn time I'll lend it to him. Next time he can go home in the dark."

With that he grabbed the lamp and disappeared out on the porch, still telling about a lot of other things he had to get done that evening.

By then the reporter decided to leave, realizing that the answer to his question was obvious. From what he had witnessed it could only be, "Keep busy!"

CHAPTER THIRTY-NINE

FINDERS KEEPERS

Lost mines are rather common in almost any other state where a large amount of mining and prospecting has been done. I've often wondered why Alaska, where so many people have mined for gold, didn't create a bunch of lost gold mines. It must be due to the fact that most old sourdoughs were not the type to lose anything, once they had found it.

For one thing, they had to be healthy, strong and level-headed to go out into an unexplored country and blaze their way through. To where? They didn't know. That in itself may have given them a lot of drive, wondering what would be around the next bend in the river, or how far it was to that range of hills where they might find gold in the stream gravel.

The oldest old-timers and trail blazers way back in the 1880's and 1890's were the boys who explored this country when it was really touch-and-go. I am willing to bet that those boys didn't grow up with an ice cream cone

159

in one hand, a bottle of pop in the other, and a tv set in front of them. I sometimes sort of pat myself on the back and tell myself that I am a real old sourdough. After all, I am not exactly a newcomer. But when I see the evidence way out there in the hills of what those old boys had to do in certain places, I kind of feel like a little boy on his first day in school. The work they left behind them tells me in plain language that they were not quitters or they would never have got out there in the first place.

What did they do that we can't do? Almost everything! Now, I have no intention of belittling the present generation or any part of it. But we all have to fit in with the time in which we happen to belong, and time is forever changing. So when I say that almost anything they did, very few of you could do now, I mean just that. And yet when I say that you could have done the same things if your way of life had demanded it, you might doubt it. But you could and you would if the *urge for adventure* was in your blood.

A typical story of how these tough men came to Alaska to find the mines they wouldn't let go of, would run something like this. A new rumor comes out that there is a strong possibility of rich deposits of placer gold in the Alaska Range. Nobody really knows for sure, but indications from reliable sources are very encouraging.

Twelve young men get together and decide to gamble on it. There are no roads, no planes, nothing at all in the way of transportation, except steamboats. So they board a steamboat in Seattle, bringing along at least a year's supplies. They don't forget anything, for necessities of every kind will be hard to get on the Alaskan coast, and awfully high-priced. In the Alaska Range itself, nothing can be purchased.

It's about mid-winter, and the boys land in Valdez. They are a healthy bunch and plenty smart. They brought everything: dogs, sleds, guns, and lots of ammunition, fishing tackle, and so on. They have enough to last them for at least a year. They don't have any experience freighting with dogs, but they start in over the Valdez Glacier.

It is necessary for them to do their hauling in relays, which means running back and forth a few miles at a time, until everything is brought to the relay cache. Then they start from there again and relay it ahead a few miles farther, and set up a new camp there. And so on ahead from one relay camp to the next. Finally, they arrive at their destination in the Alaska Range, where their gleaming pay-streak is at the bottom of some mountain stream, waiting for them to come and dig it out.

After the first hundred miles, however, there are only eight of the original group left—the other four turned back. The eight will make it, they are dog mushers by now. They found out that if they let the dogs have their way, they'd never get there. But the eight are made out of the kind of stuff that will stop for nothing. They really have what it takes, and are glad that the other four boys went back, because they were always beefing about something, anyway.

Well, there you have it. I don't think I need to go any farther. You can see what I mean now. How many of you would want to tackle a deal like that? And how many of you could do it?

Remember, there are no communications, no roads, no planes, nobody is going to keep an eye on you from the air. If anything goes wrong, you can't call anyone on a walkie-talkie and say: "Come in with a helicopter. Joe Wilson broke his leg." You are strictly on your own. Nobody even knows where you are or what you are doing.

You can just about see a picture of it now. Even if you could do it today, it wouldn't make sense. But those old boys back then didn't have any choice. The type that would turn back sorted themselves out along the trail, which automatically put a bunch of men out in the field that were not the type of men to find a rich mine and then lose it again. Of course, some of them did lose the *gold* after they dug it out, but they lost it across the poker table or to roulette wheels. After all, many of them were gamblers. And a lot of them, regardless of how big, strong, husky and healthy they were, showed their weakness when they got around to where there were women. But they didn't lose the location of their claim.

Further proof of the strong character of these old-timers is the evidence of work left by them throughout Alaska.

I've run across some of the real old log houses and cabins built by men who came to the interior of Alaska just the way I mentioned, over the Valdez Glacier. Looking at the remains of those old houses now, I can almost hear the old-timers' voices saying: "This is the only home we have, so we'll put in all our effort to make a real home of it." The only tools most of them had were a good ax and a drawknife. Nails and spikes were pretty scarce, so they had augers and braces and bits in all sizes. They also had broadaxes, and they knew how to use them. I've seen the walls on some of those old log houses out there in places, hewed so smooth they looked like solid board walls.

They must have spent the long winter evenings making wooden pegs or pins. Almost everything was pinned to-

162

gether with pins made of spruce wood or birch. The gable logs had been pinned together, pins and pegs were fastened on the wall to hang clothes on, and beds were made out of straight, round peeled spruce poles pinned together. Doors were made the same way, with hinges made out of birch. The hole that the pin of the hinge was fitted into was lined with rawhide, which they would grease once in a while with hot tallow to keep it from squeaking, and wearing out. In some of the log houses, they had big windows and even double windows for the winter months. Frames were made out of hewed spruce poles and snugly fitted. Instead of glass, they used white linen or flour sacks sealed with paraffin.

They made candle molds out of wood with brace and bit or small augers. They made candles out of caribou and moose tallow. In places where they could get big slabs of shale, they built fine cook stoves and chimneys. And all out of rocks! They also built heaters and fireplaces out of rocks, using glacier muck, which is a sticky blue clay, and usually stands the heat pretty good if a small portion of sand is mixed with it. In some places the clay had to be hauled a long distance.

They kept whatever number of dogs they had to have, and no more. They had drying rocks and smokehouses for curing meat. If they didn't have a whipsaw, they usually knew where they could borrow one.

When they decided to make lumber, they would get together and help each other, as it takes two men to saw lumber. When they found gold bearing gravel good enough to sluice, they needed lots of lumber for boxes. If it was necessary, they would keep that whipsaw going night and day, taking turns on it. While each man might own his individual claim, they had to help each other in a lot of different ways. One of them might be a crackerjack at building fireplaces, rock stoves, heaters and chimneys. Others were handy at making furniture out of young, straight spruce poles. They traded work with each other, and lived in comfort by making use of what nature provided for them.

No doubt a lot of them had quite a sense of humor. In one old cabin on the Lower Beaver Creek, somebody had gone to considerable trouble to make a sign which hung right over the door. It read: "Everything is free here. And if you are not satisfied, you get your money back."

In one of the old cabins along the Forty Mile River, I found an old diary. It had been wet and it was hard to make out. But a few pages were very plain. The year marked on it was 1902. One of the entries read: "Mail brought to me by John Madsen, had letter from my sweet little wife. Said she will come up here in the spring and bring my two little jewels, Carl and Betty. Never been so happy in my life! Whoopee!"

And the next one: "Didn't sleep much last night. Kept thinking about Mama, Carl and Betty. Hope they like it here. Am not worried about money, since I found that pay on the bench. Getting sleepy now. Hope I can sleep tonight. Good night, Mama, Carl, and Betty. I love you all."

Well, I kind of got off the track. I intended to write about lost mines. And I think I've made it plain enough for you to see why those old boys didn't walk away and leave a rich gold mine in some part of the country where they couldn't find it again. I believe there are some very rich mines up here in places, all right. But they are *not lost.* They haven't even been found yet. They're just lying there, waiting for somebody with curiosity and guts to come and find them.

CHAPTER FORTY

THE SEARCH

The search for the unknown will always continue. It appears to be the game of life. We're all in it, but naturally we're not all searching for the same thing. Alaska is full of surprises, and nobody knows what somebody will run into next. Not long ago they discovered the big oil field in the Arctic. It wouldn't surprise me a bit if someday soon, some old ball came out of the wilderness, walked into a jewelry shop, showed the jeweler a poke full of small flakes and pieces of dull silvery looking iron or steel, but awful heavy. The jeweler would tell him, "No wonder it's heavy, this is platinum. If you didn't stake the ground where you found this, you better keep your mouth shut and get back out there and stake what claims you want for yourself. You are a rich man! Even the poke you have there is worth five thousand dollars."

While it is true that there is hardly anybody out prospecting in the field any more, the unexpected happens sometimes, and something like this could happen to someone with a curious nature. As a free man out there in the free and open, following one's curiosity becomes a grand game with nature, and if the player enjoys the game for the sake of playing, he can't really lose. He may find a fortune, and if he does, he is a big winner. If he fails to find anything, well, he enjoyed the game, so it's a fair gamble.

So the search goes on and on, not only out in the wilderness, but at sea, in the air, in the whole universe. The only way the search can make progress is through man's free mind on any frontier. Through natural impulses, something within the mind of man keeps him wondering what's under that overburden of soil, around the next bend in the river, or way out there in the middle of the Milky Way. And whatever it is that appeals to him, leave him alone to have at it, and he'll get there. Freedom is the passkey to any frontier, and I was lucky to have followed my curiosity to Alaska when it was free.